A STUDY OF LONERGAN'S SELF-TRANSCENDING SUBJECT AND KEGAN'S EVOLVING SELF

A STUDY OF LONERGAN'S SELF-TRANSCENDING SUBJECT AND KEGAN'S EVOLVING SELF
A Framework for Christian Anthropology

Robert Berchmans

Roman Catholic Studies
Volume 14

The Edwin Mellen Press
Lewiston•Queenston•Lampeter

Library of Congress Cataloging-in-Publication Data

Berchmans, Robert.
   A study of Lonergan's self-transcending subject and Kegan's evolving self : a
framework for Christian anthropology / Robert Berchmans.
      p. cm. -- (Roman Catholic studies ; v. 14)
   Includes bibliographical references and index.
   ISBN 0-7734-7382-3
   1. Man (Christian theology) 2. Lonergan, Bernard J.F. 3. Kegan, Robert. 4. Catholic
Church--Doctrines. I. Title. II. Series.

BT701.3 .B47 2001
233--dc21
                                                                    2001024001

This is volume 14 in the continuing series
Roman Catholic Studies
Volume 14 ISBN 0-7734-7382-3
RCS Series ISBN 0-88946-240-X

A CIP catalog record for this book is available from the British Library.

The Edwin Mellen Press   The Edwin Mellen Press
Box 450   Box 67
Lewiston, New York   Queenston, Ontario
USA 14092-0450   CANADA L0S 1L0

The Edwin Mellen Press, Ltd.
Lampeter, Ceredigion, Wales
UNITED KINGDOM SA48 8LT

Printed in the United States of America

Dedicated to

My parents, Professor and Mrs. Berchmans
My wife, Charmaine
My children, Danielle and Everette

TABLE OF CONTENTS

PREFACE

This book arises from the author's conviction that there is a lacuna in contemporary Catholic moral theology. Berchmans holds that today's Catholic moral theology, despite its mostly positive thrust, has retained a flawed point of departure in its Christian anthropology. In the aftermath of the Second Vatican Council, a concerted effort on the part of moral theologians such as Bernard Häring and Josef Fuchs moved away from the manualist tradition characteristic of pre-conciliar Catholic moral theology. Berchmans contends that the vestiges of the manualist tradition can still be clearly seen in contemporary Catholic moral theology. He points out that this involves what he calls "a cognitive entrapment" in an inadequate anthropology. Instead of regarding the human person as a unity, post-conciliar moral theology has continued to make regular reference to the various faculties of body, mind, will, etc. It thus seems unable to move out of the framework of faculty psychology.

The purpose of Berchmans's study is to steer away from a Christian anthropology based in faculty psychology and to offer an alternate framework. In this framework, the human subject is presented in the light of human existence as it is experienced in the ever-unfolding mystery of transcendence-in-immanence.

The inspiration for this framework comes from Max Scheler and Maurice Blondel. Both were critical of perspectives that see the human subject as a collection of faculties. They claimed that we must no longer regard the human in terms of a two-tiered compartment of nature and supernature and argued, instead, for both the unity of the human experience subject and the unity of human experience.

To present this alternate framework, Berchmans employs a method of dialogue. He draws together the works of the theologian Bernard Lonergan and the psychologist Robert Kegan in an engaging fashion to provide the framework for a Christian anthropology that links meaning to self-transcendence. The meaning that is central to Kegan's theory is rooted in self-transcendence, while the self-transcendence central to Lonergan's thinking cannot achieved without the subject seeking meaning in the sensory, cognitive, affective and religious realms. By developing lines of connection between Kegan's concept of meaning and Lonergan's notion of self-transcendence, the author leads us to an enriched understanding of what it means to be human.

A refreshing feature of this study is that Berchmans does not confine his discussion to the western thought traditions represented by the two major thinkers he explores her. He gives a prominent place to ideas of *imago dei* and *theosis* that complement his main thesis and enable him to enter into the rich heritage of the traditions of Eastern Christianity.

Berchmans's work makes a significant contribution by taking an honest look at issues and challenges that face contemporary Christian anthropology. It brings to the surface a range of poignant questions that Christian anthropology must address. Among the crucial issues brought into the discussion are: the dichotomization of the human (nature/supernature; grace/nature; boudy/soul; matter/spirit;), the polarization of the human (male/female), the fragmentation of the human (body/soul/mind/will/matter/spirit), the reification of sin and grace, the particularization and separation of human origin from the rest of creation, and the localization of human destiny. The framework presented in this study is meant to bring about a healthy response to each of these issues and challenges.

Berchmans's work not only offers a major contribution to the field of Christian anthropology; it should also have repercussions for discussions in Catholic moral theology. It brings a refreshing outlook to the question of what it means to be human. It emphasizes that to be human is to strive for self-transcendence and that his self-transcendence cannot be achieved if the human is dichotomized, polarized or fragmented. Berchmans challenges Christian anthropologists to hearken to the single thrust towards self-transcendence that provides the trajectory for what it means to be human.

Philip Rossi, S.J.

CHAPTER I
A FRAMEWORK FOR CHRISTIAN ANTHROPOLOGY

1. INTRODUCTION

1.1. Renewal in Catholic Theology

Contemporary Catholic theology has come a long way since the beginning of the twentieth century. At the turn of the century, the official Church had made it clear that Catholic theology had necessarily to be framed in the context of one philosophical system, Scholasticism. It was merely a reiteration of the Church's position spelled out in the nineteenth century by Leo XIII in his encyclical *Aeterni Patris*. One of the reasons why Pius X was unequivocal in condemning the Modernists in his encyclical *Lamentabili* was because the Modernists, especially thinkers like Lucien Laberthonniere, had posed a strong threat to Scholasticism. It was not until Vatican II that the theological monolithic edifice built on one single system of thought would come to be considered one among numerous other viable systems of thought that could be used to explore and to interpret the interaction of God with creation.[1]

The fresh air surging through the window opened by Pope John XXIII with the Second Vatican Council was particularly refreshing to Catholic theology. *Gaudium et Spes* encouraged theologians to collaborate with the secular sciences and declared that "appropriate use must be made not only of theological principles, but also of the findings of the secular sciences, especially psychology and sociology. Let them blend modern science and its theories and the understanding of the most recent discoveries with Christian morality and doctrine. Thus their morality can keep pace with their scientific knowledge and with an ever-advancing technology"[2] This ushered in a radical change in the way Catholic theology would be done from then on. This gust of fresh air has been refreshing and rejuvenating. However, we need to be cautious lest we overstate what has been achieved in the aftermath of the council.

In the past thirty years, Catholic theology has profited immensely from a healthy dialogue with modern and contemporary philosophy and various social sciences. The influence of Existentialism, Vitalism, Personalism, Marxism, Phenomenology and many other systems of thought on contemporary Catholic thinkers bears ample testimony to the radically changed landscape of Catholic theology.[3] There is a new-found latitude and depth that makes it possible to present Christianity as more viable and meaningful to post-modern Christians. There is no denying the fact that Catholic theology has made significant strides in engaging modern and contemporary philosophy as can be clearly seen in the works of Karl Rahner, Bernard Lonergan, Hans Kung, Edward Schillebeeckx, Gustavo Gutierrez[4] and a host of other Catholic thinkers.

1.2. Renewal in Catholic moral theology

Has Catholic theology engaged in a similar dialogue with human sciences, especially psychology and sociology, as was envisioned in *Gaudium et Spes*? Although an affirmative answer can be given, we have to admit that the dialogue, regrettably, has not been that significant. For the purpose of this study, we need specifically to point out the relative lack of interaction between theological anthropology and developmental psychology. It is true that paradigm shifts in culture and society has brought about significant changes in the attitude of Catholics toward sin, grace, sacraments, etc. However, theological responses to these changes of attitude have been more philosophical in nature and have scarcely been the result of meaningful dialogue between theology and psychology. Bernard Haring,[5] Josef Fuchs,[6] Enda McDonagh,[7] Charles Curran[8] and several other Catholic moral theologians have been instrumental in changing the minimalistic and legalistic tendencies of pre-Vatican II moral theology. However, their dialogue with psychology and sociology can be categorized only as tangential. Walter Conn[9] has engaged in direct and explicit dialogue with psychology. His interest has been in the area of conscience and conversion. He has done admirably in working out a meaningful dialogue between the theories of Jean Piaget, Lawrence Kohlberg, and other developmental psychologists with the notion of self-transcendence in Bernard Lonergan[10]. We need to expand the dialogue to rethink our understanding of what it means to be human. Is there a possible reason why this dialogue has not made much headway?

A principal reason why this meaningful dialogue between and theology and psychology has not taken place is that Catholic moral theology while trying to renew itself has mainly operated in the old mode of faculty psychology. Though it must be admitted that the discussion of sin and virtue has most certainly moved from particular acts to focus on the whole person, it is quite evident that the whole person is seen principally in the light of one's faculties of intellect and will. Faculty psychology entraps theological thinking in categories that block meaningful dialogue with contemporary psychology. This calls for a paradigm shift that will disengage us from faculty psychology and be rid of what can be termed "a cognitive entrapment." When that happens, we will be able to engage in dialogue with contemporary psychology and that in turn will open the doors for a radical revitalization of Catholic moral theology. What Catholic theology needs is not merely a revitalization of moral theology but a rethinking and reinterpretation of Christian anthropology. In some sense, this rethinking and reinterpretation of Christian anthropology is what this work calls for and seeks to develop.

Theologians, for the most part, have accepted that to understand and interpret the meaning and significance of the interplay between God and creation we must first and foremost understand the meaning and significance of what it means to be human. However, the crucial problem for contemporary Christian Anthropology is answering the question: What does it really mean to be human? In attempting an answer to this question we have to keep in mind that the biologist, the psychologist, the sociologist, and every human scientist has a particular understanding of what it means to be human. Does the theologian have a unique and exclusive answer or does the theologian rely on the various sciences for insights to arrive at a theological answer to the question?

2. AN ALTERNATE FRAMEWORK FOR CHRISTIAN ANTHROPOLOGY: Human finitude paradoxically open to infinite possibilities

At the heart of understanding what it means to be human is the recognition and the acceptance of the reality of human finitude that harbors within itself infinite possibilities for future growth and development. Human finitude is part and parcel of the quotidian human experience. Every human person wakes up to the reality of human limitedness. At the close of the day, it is human limitedness that seeks refreshment in slumber or forces one to drop off to sleep. There is no getting away from the experience of finitude. The most drastic experience of human finitude, without doubt, is death. Human helplessness and the acceptance of the fact that we have no ultimate control or grasp of ourselves looms large before each of us throughout our lives, even before facing the actuality of our death. In sum, finitude is quintessential to human experience.

However, to restrict the understanding of what it means to be human to the experience of human finitude would be to present a totally distorted picture of what it means to be human. From the moment we are conceived, humans are on an odyssey, a journey of immense magnitude, exploring-- and more importantly, growing with every exploration-- possibilities that far exceed the present experience of one's humanity. This growth and development takes place on one's sentient, affective, cognitive, moral, and spiritual/religious levels. This development or the moving beyond the present experience of self or this self-transcendence is as much quintessential to human experience as one's finitude.

It must be pointed out that as this self-transcendence is imbedded in one's finitude, there is the stark possibility for stunting or thwarting the possibilities for growth and development. Self-transcendence is woven into the fabric of our humanity, but it has to be realized; it has to be worked out by each individual and each community of individuals. It must be reiterated that the realization of self-transcendence, either in the individual or in the community of individuals has to take place in the context of finitude, because, as I have stated, there is no getting away from human finitude. Hence, understanding what it means to be human must necessarily be worked out in the parameters of one's self-transcendence and finitude.

This is thus offered as a study in Christian anthropology. Finitude and self-transcendence, as explained above, are not restricted to the Christian experience. This could as well be a work in general anthropology, not that the two are mutually exclusive, but there has to be a more direct justification to regard this work as a study in Christian anthropology. The experience of self-transcendence imbedded in our finitude may be expressed in Christian theological terminology as "Grace in Exile." Human persons are "bounded boundlessness"-- they are the incarnation of God's boundless grace. In other words, to understand the human person we need to place him/her in the context of his/her limited existence that is open to God's infinite possibilities. Apart from the divine grace that makes the human seek ever higher fulfillment, human existence will flounder in the quagmire of pessimistic nihilism. Apart from the realization that human existence is always a bounded existence, that is, it is a limited realization at any moment of the infinite divine possibilities, humans run the risk of irrelevance in a world that is increasingly secular. It is crucial to keep the balance between the bounded and the boundless. The tension between the finite and infinite as experienced in human existence is the arena where every dialogue in Christian anthropology must take place. This work attempts to give the basis for the suggested framework and initiate some possibilities for doing Christian anthropology that can be significant and relevant to the contemporary Christian. The thesis of this study is that the experience of finitude in human existence is paradoxically interwoven with an openness to infinite possibilities, which in fact finds its source (*imago Dei*) and destiny (*theosis*) in God himself.

3. BACKDROP FOR THE FRAMEWORK

Attempting a literature review on frameworks for doing Christian anthropology would be an exercise in futility, as we would have to cover a vast area. In the closing decades of the last century and the dawning decades of the twentieth century there were several original and creative thinkers who broke out of stagnant ways of looking at reality in general and humanity in particular. They were from differing intellectual, cultural, and religious backgrounds. They were trained in diverse disciplines. Their contributions transcended the bounds of their discipline. Their influences were far reaching. Their thoughts and works were original and, consequently, do not mirror the thoughts and works of other similar thinkers. However, it can be stated that their hearts seem to speak the same language. To name a few of those who would belong to this outstanding group: Maurice Blondel, Max Scheler, Henri Bergson, Abraham Heschel, Martin Buber, Friederick von Hugel, and Teilhard de Chardin.

What I propose to do is to single out two thinkers from those mentioned above: Maurice Blondel and Max Scheler. I consider them to be pioneers of a theological anthropology that has an integrative epistemology as its base. Like Bernard Lonergan, they believed in a single dynamism as the unifying principle in humanity. Each in his unique way developed this notion of the human person as a mystery that harbors multifarious aspects in unity. Though the framework that this work spells out is not articulated by either of these pioneers in the same way, they were two of the principal inspirations for this framework. Sketching out their thinking here would be beneficial to this work, both as a starting point and as providing a direction for the rest of the chapters.

3.1. Maurice Blondel

Maurice Blondel (1861-1949) had an extraordinarily potent and long literary and philosophical career extending over 60 years. There is a single purpose behind all his writings: there is in the human heart the search for and the need for the infinite. The opening sentence of *L'action* leaves little doubt that here we have a stimulating and engaging mind, which knew the direction of its journey: "Is it true or not that human life has meaning and man, a destiny?"[11] Much like the thesis of this work, meaning, human origin and destiny, was for Blondel the point of departure and the point of arrival.

From his *L'Action* to his final work *La Philosophie et l'Esprit chretien* Blondel expressed his lack of enthusiasm for Scholastic philosophy. He was not content with expressing his dissatisfaction with Scholasticism. He sought a solution. We can trace the beginnings of the solution in his Latin thesis, *Vinculum Substantiale*, which states convincingly that there had to be a connecting link between faith and reason, the natural and the supernatural.[12]

If Blondel was convinced that there was a connecting link between reason and faith, the natural and the supernatural, our question is what was this link. This 'vinculum substantiale' for Blondel was Action. The term "action" was non-existent in the philosophical dictionaries of his times. Even in the academic circles of Paris there was consternation. Blondel knew that he had found something original. It would be his legacy for posterity. Action, for Blondel, was the spiritual dynamism that unites thought, will, and being and opens itself to the 'ontological affirmative' which is the infinite. Action is every human activity whether it is physical, psychological, or spiritual. It is the sum total of one's inner existence. Blondel admitted that he was indebted to Spinoza and Immanuel Kant for providing inspiration for his life's work.[13]

Blondel's other major influence was Kant. Jean Lacroix points out that Blondel and Kant were of the same intention--speculative thinking cannot solve all problems. However, this is where Blondel parted company with Kant. For Blondel, Kant was not radical enough. Blondel did a critique of Kant's critique. There is something, which takes both the speculative and practical reason and brings them to a synthesis--and that synthesis is the dialectic of action. Of particular importance is what is seen as Blondel's singular contribution, his *methode d'imminence.*[14] It was the method of arriving at a solution through a dialectical synthesis. Rationalism and Idealism had driven a wedge between the natural and the supernatural. Rationalism had made it impossible to get access to the supernatural or the "the starry heaven above" as Kant would say. Idealism had concentrated on the subject so exclusively that it resulted in what Blondel termed "subjective dogmatism." It seemed as if this division between nature and supernature was irreconcilable. Blondel, on the other hand, was convinced that the infinite is to be found in everything. He called it "the cry of nature." He wrote repeatedly that there is imbedded in the whole universe a need and an upward yearning for that which is beyond. He stated in unmistakable terms that there is a necessary transcendence in everything that is immanent.

Blondel proceeded systematically to elaborate on the presence of the transcendent in the whole order of nature. He began with sentient being and moved on to science, to consciousness, to society, to human society, and to the universe. Lacroix sums it up succinctly, "It is an upward climb, some kind of journey, an ascent from being to Being."[15] Blondel has a Teilhardian ring about him.[16] In Blondel we sense a cyclical movement upward that touches everything in creation. Everything in creation was charged with the majesty of the infinite.[17] Blondel's intellectual approach, not only to philosophy and theology but also his approach to the human mystery serves as a backdrop to this study.

3.2. Max Scheler

Max Scheler (1874-1928), born of a Jewish mother and a Protestant father, repudiated his family's religious backgrounds and embraced Catholicism.[18] In his later years he abandoned all forms of traditional religion. He maintained his belief in God, though not the Judeo-Christian God. His writings are very reminiscent of Augustine and Pascal. Whereas in his earlier writings, Scheler is a personalist, a theist, and a convinced Christian, in his last work, *Die Stellung des Menschen im Kosmos*,[19] we see a profound change where he not only questions his previous faith, he even repudiates his earlier theistic orientation.

Scheler was a younger contemporary of Blondel. Among the 19th century philosophers who influenced Scheler's thinking were Nietzsche, Dilthey, and Bergson. Troeltsch even calls him 'the Catholic Nietzsche.' He studied under Rudolf Eucken and cultivated an interest in the philosophy of the spiritual life. A decisive event in Scheler's intellectual life was his meeting with Edmund Husserl. Scheler saw in Husserl's phenomenology a method for investigating human spiritual experience[20] and masterfully utilized it to serve his own purpose of studying religion and religious experience.

Scheler's first major work published in 1916 was *Der Formalismus in der Ethick and die materiale Werthethik* (Formalism in Ethics and an Ethic of Objective Values). In this work, Scheler proclaimed the simple, yet radical thesis that 'values' be given the same objective and autonomous status in nature as in sensory qualities or material objects. This is important to this work because as we shall see later Lonergan acknowledges direct indebtedness to Scheler for his notion of value. We find in Scheler a remarkable resonance of Blaise Pascal. Scheler abandoned the classical dualism of the body and soul, but posited a metaphysical dualism of life and spirit.

Throughout life one of his recurring questions was "What is man?" He devoted his life to studying and writing on philosophical anthropology much before the term became popular.[21] His last publication before his death was *Die Stellung des Menschen im Kosmos* [*Man's Place in the Universe*]. In Scheler's words, "This essay represents a brief and highly condensed summary of my view on some of the main topics of the 'Philosophical Anthropology' on which I have been at work for a number of years and which will appear early in 1929."[22] Unfortunately, Scheler died on May 13, 1928, and this work was never published. *Man's Place in the Universe* gives us an adequate picture of Scheler's religious anthropology.

Scheler espoused a dynamic and evolutionary notion of man.[23] He speaks of stages in the evolutionary development of the psyche. The lowest stage, according to him, is an undifferentiated vital impulse or drive (*Gefuhlsdrang*) which is similar to Spinoza's *connatus*, Schopenhauer's blind will, or Bergson's *elan vital. Man's Place in the Universe* makes it evident that

> Spinoza's pantheism and Bergson's creative evolution fuse in Scheler's concept of "self-deification" of man. With the death of God in the religious sense, man becomes God. Hegel's idea of the self-realization of Reason in history now appears in the context of a creative pantheism, as the self-realization of God in man and history. God is constantly "becoming" in man to the extent to which mankind realized its own

spiritual potentialities or transforms natural resources and vital energies into products of the spirit.[24]

In the fourth chapter of the *Man's Place in the Universe* which is entitled "Philosophical Anthropology and Religion" Scheler sums up some of his thoughts and these will have to suffice for our purpose here:

> The locus of this self-realization, or let us say, self-deification, as it were, for which the Being in itself strives and for the sake of which it pays the price of the world as 'history' – this locus is man, the human self and the human heart. Here is the only place where the deification is accessible to us – but it is a genuine part of the transcendent process itself, for although all things emerge in the process of continuous creation from the Ground of Being, from the functional unity of the cooperative interplay between spirit and drive, these two attributes of the Being in itself that are known to us are related to each other solely in man as a living unity. Man is the focus where they intersect.[25]

Scheler's philosophical anthropology is too complex for us to explicate in detail. However, what I have presented here should provide a glimpse into Scheler's attempt to articulate a framework that was intended as an alternative to the classical understanding of "man." Scheler wrote, "We may say that at no time in his history has man been so much of a problem to himself as he is now. For this reason I have tried to give an outline of a new philosophical anthropology based on as broad a foundation as possible."[26] In some way, the framework presented in this work is reflective of Scheler's 'outline of that new philosophical anthropology.'

4. PRELIMINARY CLARIFICATIONS

At the very outset, a few preliminary clarifications must be made. First, though this is a work in Christian anthropology, it is in no way an attempt to present a systematic or concise treatment of Christian anthropology. It is meant to be a "framework." As a framework, it is only intended as a broad outline that provides a guideline for doing Christian anthropology. Second, recent advances in biology and genetics, psychology and social anthropology, science and technology have dramatically changed the way we answer the question, "What does it mean to be human?" It would be presumptuous to suggest that we will be able to dialogue with these various disciplines in the limited scope of this study. At the very least, the framework that we present here should resonate with these various disciplines. However, we will be explicitly in dialogue with one of these disciplines, psychology, to be more precise, with one theory of developmental psychology, proposed by the Harvard psychologist, Robert Kegan. In fact, Kegan's theory of the "Evolving Self" will provide part of our argumentation and elaboration for the framework presented here. Thirdly, we will not be studying extensively what it means to be human in the Christian Scriptures. However, the framework presented here has its roots in the biblical notion that humans are created in the image and likeness of God (Gen 1: 26). The theology of *imago Dei* gives a solid foundation to this framework. Another theological basis for this framework is the notion of *theosis,* participation in the divine or deification. Fourthly, the emphasis in this work will be on self-transcendence. We will take the finitude and limitedness of the human as a given. However, when we discuss issues of origin (source) and destiny of the human, nature and supernature, we will focus on both transcendence and immanence, as the framework presented here is: Human existence is the ever-unfolding mystery of transcendence-in-immanence.

5. PROCEDURAL OUTLINE
5.1. Chapter one

After we have stated the purpose of the study and made some preliminary clarifications, we will proceed to set out the methodology of this work and the rationale for its method. After a look at two significant thinkers, Maurice Blondel and Max Scheler, who have been influential in shaping the framework for Christian anthropology offered in this study, we will then introduce the theologian Bernard Lonergan and the psychologist Robert Kegan, principally focusing on their writings and why we think their work will help to establish and elaborate the framework for Christian anthropology presented here. Finally, we will enumerate six issues and challenges which, in the opinion of the writer of this work, must be addressed in any contemporary framework for doing Christian anthropology. Although it is beyond the scope of this study to demonstrate if the framework presented satisfactorily addresses all these issues and challenges, we will point out as part of the last chapter that what we have attempted is meant as the initial work that has to be furthered in the future.

5.2. Chapter two

In chapter two, we will present Lonergan's notion of the human subject. The purpose is to bring out Lonergan's indubitable belief that the human subject cannot be understood apart from its intrinsic exigence to transcend one's present possibilities. In Lonergan's anthropology, we can speak of the human subject only in as much as we draw our understanding from its intrinsic drive to self-transcendence without which humans cannot be humans. We will also emphasize that for Lonergan, the human subject realizes itself in an ever-progressive, ever-surpassing grasp of one's self through authentic self-transcendence. In order to fulfill these objectives, we will first examine what, according to Lonergan, it means to be human. This will require a study of Lonergan's writings beginning with his earliest, tracing developments that are crucial to our study. We will thus look at his intellectual heritage and the key philosophical and psychological interlocutors who influenced him to arrive at his own notion of the human subject as self-transcendent. This chapter will fall short of a comprehensive look at Lonergan's notion of the human subject because crucial aspects of horizon and conversions will be explored in chapter 4. The second chapter gives the philosophical basis for understanding Lonergan's notion of self-transcendence and hence does not enter into the religious or the theological realms. Differing discussion of horizon and conversions to the fourth chapter will better serve the theological argument in this study.

5.3. Chapter three

Chapter three will be devoted to the study of Robert Kegan's theory of Evolving Self and how it is consonant with the notion of the human person in his/her intrinsic drive to self-transcendence. The rationale for this study, as well as its place in the work, will be explicated later in this chapter under methodological considerations. Primary attention will be devoted to Kegan's overall understanding of the ever-progressive, ever-surpassing grasp of oneself that is realized through the dynamics of the process of growing and developing throughout one's life span. In order to grasp Kegan's theory better, we will present some background for his psychological theory. Kegan considers himself a neo-Piagetian. He presents himself as taking his roots from Piaget's genetic epistemology, by which Kegan means that he inherits from Piaget, not so much Piaget's psychology, as his philosophy of how an individual arrives at knowledge and truth and more pointedly how an individual constructs meaning from one's surroundings and experiences.

We will also dwell on how Kegan considers himself as offering a third psychological tradition, the first two being the Neo-Psychoanalytic tradition and the Existential-Phenomenological tradition. He presents himself as preserving the best of these two traditions after a critical appraisal of their tenets. His theory takes the dynamism that is integral to the Neo-psychoanalytic tradition and the integrity and wholeness that is crucial to the Existential-phenomenological tradition. Kegan combines these elements with the Neo-Piagetian constructivism. Kegan claims that he brings together the two Big Ideas of developmentalism and constructivism into a unity in his theory. He presents this as Constructive-Developmentalism, the third psychological tradition.

Kegan asserts that though his theory takes the best from other theories, it is not just a juxtaposition of parts of other theories, but genuinely a new approach that has its own integrity. Kegan's theory is that humans are basically meaning-constructors. In other words, for Kegan, to be human means to be a meaning-maker. It is by constant striving to make meaning of who we are that we evolve as a person. This evolution of one's self-understanding through constant meaning-construction is a life-long process. As this process of meaning-making takes place in stages throughout one's life, it is a stage theory. A stage theory proposes a sequential development that takes place in stages, each stage with its own nature and structure. To understand Kegan's theory, we will explain his five-stage theory elaborating on the nature and development of each of those stages. A decade after Kegan presented his theory in *The Evolving Self*, Kegan wrote *In Over Our Heads*. We will make some salient comments on his later work that relates to his theory. We will critique his theory. The conclusion to the chapter will center on the theme of self-transcendence and what role Kegan's theory will play in the establishment of the thesis of the work.

5.4. Chapter four

In the second and third chapters, we focused on self-transcendence in the works of Lonergan and Kegan. However, in both the chapters we restricted our discussion to self-transcendence that was limited to the empirical realm. By that I mean that in regard to Lonergan we confined ourselves to self-transcendence in the plane of experience, knowledge, judgment, and values and in regard to Kegan we limited ourselves to psychological development that did not bring in the religious or spiritual dimensions which are beyond the empirical realm. In the fourth chapter, we will show that though Kegan as a psychologist had to limit his inquiry to the empirical, his first published work, *Sweeter Welcome*, provides us with some clues with which to address the ontological questions that human self-transcendence necessarily raises. We will argue that Kegan's psychological theory can be meaningfully placed in the larger context of his writings, which in turn will be linked to the theological framework that we are presenting in this work. Then, Lonergan's notion of horizons and conversions will be discussed. We will show how human self-transcendence has its source as well as its destiny in God.

5.5. Chapter five

The final chapter will further explore the notion of human self-transcendence as being rooted in God and searching for ultimate fulfillment in God. We will explore the theological notions of *imago Dei*, and *theosis*. This will help us articulate the theological framework for doing anthropology; namely, the human person cannot be understood except as self-transcendence in human finitude which is rooted in the notions of *imago dei* and *theosis*. We will then show how this theological framework can be used to work out a consistent contemporary Christian anthropology. We will deal with dichotomization and polarization of humanity and human destiny. The purpose of this section will be to show how the presented framework can be applied to these critical areas in Christian anthropology. They are not meant as full fledged treatments of these themes, but a demonstration of how we hope to work these themes in greater detail in the future.

6. METHODOLOGICAL CONSIDERATIONS

6.1. Theology and Psychology

As I have already pointed out, though this is a work in Christian anthropology, we will be devoting considerable energy and space to link the discussion to psychology or to be more accurate to one of the theories of ego development that has been proposed by Robert Kegan. Here we need to deal with a few methodological questions. Are we using psychology as a building block for our theology? Are we looking to psychology to get affirmation for the theological framework presented here? Do we regard psychology and theology as partners in the same search for what makes humans to be humans? To an extent, the answer to each of the questions is a qualified yes and a qualified no. First and foremost, in this work, we affirm the independence of both the disciplines. As such, there is no suggestion that psychology is simply used to serve the purposes of theology. The basis for the framework presented here is psychological to the extent that the human experience of finitude and self-transcendence are empirical and are derived from psychology. It is also theological because the experience of self-transcendence in human finitude is grounded in the biblical traditions of *imago dei* and the Christian theological tradition of *theosis* or divine participation.

Lonergan's notion of the human subject is presented in chapter two, prior to the chapter dealing with Kegan's theory, to emphasize the fact that we are not using psychology as the ancilla. It is also intended to preserve the independence of both the disciplines. In chapter 2, we explore Lonergan's writings to understand his notion of the human subject. We will find that for Lonergan the drive to self-transcendence is intrinsic to being human. Kegan's theory is presented in chapter 3 in its own right. We attempt to ascertain what this psychological theory offers us by way of understanding what it means to be human. Both Lonergan and Kegan are presented here as pursuing the same goal: to understand what it means to be human. They both explore human subjectivity. This is the rationale for choosing these two thinkers as the principal contributors to working out the framework presented here.

6.2. Lonergan and Kegan

Though both Lonergan and Kegan explore human subjectivity, they do so from two distinct perspectives. For Lonergan, one's humanity is realized in authentic self-transcendence. For Kegan, to be human means to be a meaning-maker. It is the contention of this work that both these perspectives are in fact holding the same view about what it means to be human. For Kegan, it is only through the process of meaning-making that an individual evolves; in other words, the only way humans transcend their present stage or state of humanity is by meaning-construction. If to be human means to be a meaning-maker, it is through meaning-making that one becomes more and more authentically human. Thus, we cannot speak of self-transcendence without speaking of meaning-making and vice-versa. Kegan, at least as far as his psychological theory goes, limits himself to the empirical realm and employs a psychological language. Lonergan, on the other hand, writes as a philosopher and a theologian and in keeping with these disciplines, he speaks of self-transcendence.

6.3. An Integrative Epistemology

In an article entitled "Integrative Epistemology and the Search for Meaning," LeRon Shults points out that a dualistic epistemology that has compartmentalized various disciplines into the arts and the sciences, from the time of the Enlightenment culminating in early twentieth-century positivism, has to be overcome, and his proposal is to work out an integrative epistemology. He is convinced that "The emergence of an integrative epistemology through interdisciplinary dialogue may assist in healing this dualism, illustrated in the convergence of kinetic thinking in theology, natural science and other disciplines."[27] The kinetic concept that Shults offers for the convergence of various disciplines is the concept of the "creaturely search for meaning." Shults contends that "The emergence of an integrative epistemology is evident in the growing dialogue between theology and natural sciences, which have developed conceptual frameworks to incorporate the current epistemological resolution."[28] This is what we are attempting in this work by bringing the works of Kegan and Lonergan to provide an integrative epistemology that will facilitate a better understanding of what it means to be human. The manner in which the work of Kegan and Lonergan are brought together in this work is precisely what Shults has in mind when he speaks of the interdisciplinary dialogue and the kinetic concept of the "creaturely search for meaning." Shults writes,

> The goal of integrative epistemology is not to collapse all disciplines into one great all-encompassing Science. Rather, it is to identify similarities in the learning and knowing modes of the arts and sciences, recognizing that all inquiry is pursued in relation to the same structures of spatio-temporal reality. The rationale which informs this essay is a dialectical strategy in which the creaturely inquirer's search for the *logos* (meaning) is posited as an organizing center around which the domain-specific efforts and findings of the arts and sciences discover their fulfillment within the larger activity of the human quest for the ultimate meaning or *Logos* of Creation.[29]

Each discipline yields new insights into the paradox and the mystery of the human. As Oskar Gruenwald puts it, "When light is refracted through a prism, it yields a spectrum of colors. The spectrum of all the arts and sciences, when combined, also yields new insights and clearly marks the pathways to God's creation."[30] Kegan and Lonergan present us with two perspectives on the same question: what does it mean to be human. Their views complement each other.

6.4. Jean Piaget's Influence on Kegan and Lonergan

The work of Jean Piaget serves as the inspiration for both Kegan and Lonergan. Though Kegan is a psychologist and draws directly from Piaget's work, he is quick to point out that his reliance is on Piaget's genetic epistemology rather than just his developmental cognitive psychology. By this Kegan does not intend to minimize his indebtedness or allegiance to Piaget. He identifies himself as a neo-Piagetian. Lonergan has in several places in his works acknowledged that he borrowed Piaget's psychological insights and expanded and elaborated on them significantly to work out the philosophical and theological meaning of self-transcendence. Lonergan sees the intimate connection between self-transcendence and meaning. It is only through the raising of significant questions that one finds meaningful answers. This heuristic process of question and meaningful responses in turn brings about a significant shift in one's horizon. When this shift in horizon, also called conversion, takes place, there is some measure of actualization of the subject's self-transcendence.

For Kegan, to be human means to be a meaning-maker. In discussing Kegan's theory, we understand that humans are from their birth on a journey of discovery, a discovery that is on-going, progressive and seemingly without a closure. There is an intimate connection between meaning-making and the journey of self-discovery. Progress on this journey is dependent on the meaning one makes of the self while interacting with one's environment. For Lonergan, the human is *homo viator*; s/he is on a journey from God returning back to God. This journey is successful to the extent that one experiences conversions at the intellectual, moral, affective, and religious levels. It is, in fact, the purpose of the human journey to be consumed by "an other-worldly falling in love" which is for Lonergan, the experience of religious conversion.

In the context of this study, it must be pointed out James Fowler and Walter Conn have made significant contributions to this interdisciplinary dialogue between psychology and theology. Conn's work needs particular mention here because what he has done especially in his *Conscience: Development and Self-Transcendence* and *Conscience and Conversion* is very similar to the work being undertaken here. Moreover, in these two works, Conn brings the works of Jean Piaget, Lawrence Kohlberg, and Erik Erikson into dialogue with Bernard Lonergan's notion of self-transcendence. In *Conscience and Conversion*, Conn also refers to the work of Robert Kegan. In fact, Conn cites Kegan as the one who brings the thoughts of the other psychologists together and holds him to be more complete in resonating with the notion of self-transcendence in Lonergan. Though Conn has masterfully brought the above mentioned psychologists and the works of Lonergan into fruitful dialogue, it is my contention that Conn restricts the idea of self-transcendence to the confines of conscience. Lonergan himself expressed his agreement with Conn's interpretation of his thoughts. The present work, as pointed out earlier, seeks not to limit self-transcendence to any one aspect of the human person but to the entire human person. To speak of the self-transcendence of the human subject only in terms of conscience does not do justice to the inexhaustible openness that is the human person.   Conn's work, though commendable, has been too narrow in focus. It has confined human self-transcendence to the study of conscience and conversion. Kegan's psychological theory and Lonergan's philosophical-theological notion of the human subject present self-transcendence as what it means to be human. They do not limit self-transcendence to the domain of conscience or the experience of conversion. The contribution of this work is that it emphasizes self-transcendence and finitude as the core experiences of being human. Self-transcendence, as well as limitedness, are what make us human. In other words, to be human is to be "bounded boundlessness" and not merely restrict one's self-transcendence to the phenomenon of conscience.

7. ISSUES AND CHALLENGES FOR CONTEMPORARY CHRISTIAN ANTHROPOLOGY

The history of Christian theology reveals a recurrent tendency to polarize realities in the human, such as body and spirit, matter and spirit, cognition and volition, etc. The language when speaking of these realities has tended to give them a reality and an existence of their own. As a consequence, for the most part the human person as presented in the history of Christian anthropology has been dichotomized and polarized. There have been several significant attempts, notably, the *Theologie Nouvelle*, which have attempted to integrate rather than dichotomize or polarize the human person.

We want to point out that the tendency to dichotomize and polarize the human is still present in contemporary theology. In attempting to present a framework for doing Christian anthropology, we need to be conscious of numerous ways in which these dichotomizing and polarizing tendencies present a real challenge. We will elaborate on some of these dichotomized and polarized realities: Nature-Supernature dichotomy, polarization of the human into male and female, fragmentation of the human into mind, body, matter, will, soul, etc., reification of grace and sin, particularization and separation of human origin from the rest of creation, and localization of human destiny. These issues which are at the heart of Christian anthropology have ramifications for every branch of theology.

We have specifically chosen Lonergan and Kegan because as we shall show, both Lonergan and Kegan provide us an anthropology, which is integrating rather than dichotomizing. To address the shortcomings of prior Christian anthropologies, Lonergan and Kegan offer us an anthropology that is integral and holistic. It is not the purpose of this work to lay out the detail of their integrating anthropology, but to arrive at the framework presented in this work. We shall now present some of the polarities and dichotomies that have surfaced in Christian history and return to some of them in the concluding chapter to indicate that the framework presented here can address these challenges meaningfully.

7.1 Dichotomization of the human: Nautral/Supernatural; Grace/Nature; Body/Soul; Matter/Spirit; etc.

Though Catholic theology throughout the centuries has attempted to avoid a dualistic view of the human, there is always a lurking separation of the natural and the supernatural, grace and nature, body and soul, matter and spirit. The early Church combated radical forms of dualism in the cosmological (God and the world), anthropological (Body and soul), and theological (grace and nature, sin and grace) arenas as can be seen in the manner in which Gnosticism, Marcionism and Manichaeanism were encountered.[31] The same attitude is exhibited in the Church's approach to Albigensian and Waldensian heresies in the Middle Ages. However, the Church was also careful not to collapse the separation between God and the creatures. Unfortunately, sometimes this separation has resulted in an unhealthy dichotomy between nature and supernature.

Even the word "nature" is a multileveled notion. Originally, its use in Christian theology was almost exclusively tied up with the medieval concept of nature as it was used in metaphysics. Its anthropological use as in "human nature" was a corollary to the Christological use as in "the human and divine nature in Christ." In order to understand the human nature of Christ, the nature of human beings became the center of focus.

In the history of Christian theology there has also been the tension between nature and grace which found various expressions in response to the challenges of the times. Tertullian was the first to refer to nature and grace. However, it was during the debate with Pelagius that Augustine wrote that human nature has been totally corrupted by original sin. Aquinas did admit the goodness of nature, but he regarded grace as an addition to nature, which brings nature to perfection.[32] Martin Luther looked on nature as depraved and only the grace of Christ could redeem it. In post-Tridentine Scholasticism, we hear of *natura pura*, *natura lapsa*, *natura elevata*, *natura reparata*, *natura glorificata*, etc. Grace in both Reformed theology and Catholic theology was seen as being extrinsic to nature. *Theologie nouvelle*, represented by theologians like Henri de Lubac, insisted on emphasizing the supernatural as a condition of concrete humankind.[33]

From the time of Augustine, the relationship between nature and grace has been hotly debated over the centuries. Any framework for doing Christian anthropology should be mindful of this debate and how it can be best addressed.

7.2. Polarization of the human: Male/Female

In speaking of the human understanding of God's interaction with creation, Christian theology has far too often been one-sided. In a male-dominated world, human experience was identified with the male experience. Rita Gross has pointed out that most religions and historians of religions are "intensely and unconsciously androcentric in outlook."[34] Simone de Beauvoir in her preface to *The Second Sex* reports how the dominant patriarchal culture held "man" to represent the positive and the neutral, while "woman" to represent the negative; man as the universal term to refer to human beings, woman to designate only women; man as the absolute subject, the paradigmatic human and woman as the "other."[35] Christianity rose out of Judaism, which for the most part was highly patriarchal and hierarchical. Elizabeth Schussler Fiorenza points out that "Texts and historical sources--Jewish as well as Christian--must be read as androcentric texts."[36] Anne Carr traces two traditions in early Christianity,[37] one that points to Jesus' own innovation in relation to women in treating them as disciples and equals and the other that became dominant in the patristic period which frequently described women as the symbols of evil, sexuality, matter, and sin, dualistically opposed to the good, spirit, mind, and virtue symbolized by the male.[38] Several other Jewish and Christian feminist theologians [39] have drawn attention to the fact that any contemporary framework for doing Christian anthropology will have to be holistic rather than androcentric. The human perspective, rather than the human as polarized in the male and the female should inform the way we do Christian anthropology.

7.3. Fragmentation of the human: Body/Soul/Mind/Will/Matter/Spirit

The human has been a puzzle unto him/herself. Is it the visible form, the physical body that we identify as constituting our humanity? Is it that which leaves the body at death, the soul or the spirit that makes us human? Is it rather an elusive consciousness that constitutes humanity? Is it the will that makes us who we are? Is it the mind or the brain that essentially defines our humanity? Or are we a conglomeration or a juxtapositioning of these various parts? The Buddha situated the self in one's consciousness. Aristotle saw the body as being informed by the soul. Descartes spoke of matter and spirit as essentially two separate entities. The Empiricists reduced humanity to sensual experiences. The Rationalists gave primacy to thought and rationality. Schopenhauer and Nietzsche held that thought is at the service of the will. Because the human is a complex phenomenon, it is an easy trap to fragment the human into various components. We can easily give into the fragmentation of the human forgetting the integrity and unity of the self. The human person is an integrated whole.

The human person or the self, as this work insists, is to be seen as an entity and a process that are not mutually exclusive. Corporeality is not something that we possess. It is what we are. Rahner, Schillebeeckx, and Macquarrie talk about embodiment as one of the essential characteristics of being human. The body is not a vehicle of our humanity; it is integral to our humanity. The mind or consciousness is not some ethereal substance that resides in a container. The soul is not a prisoner in the body waiting to be released. Any contemporary framework for doing Christian anthropology must enhance the unity and integrity of the human person.

7.4. Reification of Grace and Sin

The biblical understanding of grace (*charis*) is "the freely bestowed personal favor of God."[40] Paul emphasizes the absolute gift character of grace. Grace ultimately is God himself freely given or bestowed upon the whole of creation. Unfortunately, in the time prior to the Protestant Reformation, the notion of grace became greatly distorted as a "thing" that could be dispensed or distributed by the Church and bought with money by
the faithful for one's own self or for dear ones who had died. Though the predominant understanding of grace in the Catholic Church has always been

God's bountiful gift freely given to the creatures, the distinctions between *gratia creata* and *gratia increata* only made it easier to think of grace as a thing that is given. The buying and selling of indulgences and the granting of partial and plenary indulgences were clear instances of the impoverishment of the biblical understanding of grace. It is not uncommon to hear of the grace that is poured into our souls when we receive the Sacraments. When grace is thus reified, the personal, dynamic, communitarian nature of grace is rendered static, accidental, and an individual possession.

Reification of grace is more clearly evident in Catholic thinking and practices than the reification of sin. It must be admitted there is also a danger of representing sin as a thing we do. Sin is not something we do. It is rather a qualitative change in the relationship with others: God, fellow human beings and fellow creatures.

A framework for doing Christian anthropology must present grace and sin in the context of relationships with God and the rest of creation. And make that relationship to be intrinsic to the understanding what it means to be human and how one enhances or diminishes one's humanity.

7.5. Particularization and separation of human origin from the rest of creation

It was not easy for the Church to accept when Copernicus, Kepler and Galileo challenged the geocentric cosmology because it seemed to undermine the Church's belief that everything in creation was made by God to be subservient to humans. If the earth were not the center of the universe, wouldn't the central place of humans in creation be in jeopardy? The Church found Charles Darwin's theory of evolution to be untenable because according to the prevailing biblical scholarship, it contradicted what was clearly described in the Genesis creation stories. The relationship of humans to the rest of creation was presented as one of sovereignty. Humans were created as the pinnacle of creation and the human task was to dominate the rest of creation. All of creation was seen to be at the service of humanity. Contemporary science has made extraordinary advances in trying to understand the origin and development of the universe. In the macrocosm we know from Edwin Hubble's discovery that ours is not the only galaxy in the universe and that the whole universe is expanding.[41] Scientists began to ask themselves serious questions about the possibility of extra-terrestrial intelligent life forms. At the level of the microcosm, quantum mechanics has opened yet another universe by itself. Whether it is at the level of microcosm of the atom or the macrocosm of the expanding universe, the way we look at the origin and purpose of humans has to be revisited.

A framework for doing Christian anthropology has to be open to a new way of looking at human origin and human relationship to the rest of creation. To begin with, it must be open to see the relationship with creation as one of mutuality and interdependence. What it means to be human in the contemporary world will have to be defined by this mutuality and interdependence. Any framework for doing Christian anthropology must be capable of incorporating an ecotheology.

7.6. Localization of human destiny

"Eschatology has been usually described as the study of the four last things: death, judgement, heaven, and hell, which have become known as the *eschata*."[42] Catholics who for the most part have been brought up in this idea of the *eschata* are prone to think of heaven as a blissful place of rest, hell as a dreadful environment of fire and horror, and purgatory as a temporary and transitional stop for punishment, restitution and purification. The term 'beatific vision' used to refer to the reward of the just has a strong suggestion of an exquisite ocular delight. "Classical eschatology appears to claim too much and seems far too certain on matters of detail."[43] There is also a tendency on the part of many people to think of eschatology exclusively in terms of life after death. It is of paramount importance to think of eschatology as being at least as much about life before death as it is about what happens after death. We need to reclaim the biblical emphasis on the *eschaton* (Christ) and not be narrowly focused on the *eschata*. God is the ultimate destiny of humans. God is the ultimate hope.

Problems with eschatology have their roots in faulty Christian anthropology. To articulate a meaningful eschatology we must necessarily start with a framework for doing Christian anthropology that is mindful of the pitfalls like the ones that I have enumerated in this section. In the words of Dermot Lane:

> The self is under critical scrutiny in contemporary thought from a variety of sources: feminism, ecology and cosmology. These difficulties with anthropology in turn are inhibiting contemporary efforts to reconstruct a viable eschatology. For example, classical dualist anthropologies of the body and soul as well as modern anthropologies of the independent self-sufficient subject are perceived to be antithetical to the development of a social eschatology. On the other hand, collectivist anthropologies of the Marxist type or other utopian visions lose sight of the dignity of the individual and the possibility of a personal eschatological destiny. Is there a way forward out of this impasse? Is it possible to discern the outline of an alternative anthropology?[44]

8. CONCLUSION

In conclusion, I would like to reiterate that while promoting a healthy conversation between psychology and theology through the works of Kegan and Lonergan, I will attempt to present an alternative to the predominant framework used in current Christian anthropology, i.e., faculty psychology. This framework presents the human person from a holistic perspective: the human person is an inexhaustible mystery of bounded boundlessness; a tangible experience that points to limitless possibilities for the future; the immeasurable grace of God that is at home in a fragile but god-like creature, one in search of meaning, one who cannot be satisfied except in the Ultimate Meaning, the only human destiny, God.

CHAPTER II

SUBJECT AS SELF-TRANSCENDENT

1. INTRODUCTION

1.1. Exploration of the range of human subjectivity

There can be little doubt that Lonergan, by the sheer range of his interests, the breadth and depth of his writings, and the acuteness of his analysis, synthesis, and integration of various fields of knowledge, has come to exert an enormous influence on contemporary thinkers across the disciplines.[45] Vernon Gregson asserts that Lonergan's influence in theology is comparable only to that of Karl Rahner.[46] After acknowledging the importance of Lonergan and his writings, it must be noted that any serious reader of Lonergan would detect that there are significant differences between his earlier writings[47] and his later writings[48]. This is to be expected as his work stretches over a period of four decades[49] and there is substantial development in thought and style over that period of time. However, it is equally clear that the entire corpus of Lonergan's writings has a unity of focus -- human subjectivity. This exploration of the range of human subjectivity was most definitely shaped and formed by the influences and the stage of his intellectual development. Lonergan's earlier works reflect his scholastic, and more precisely Thomistic moorings, while his later works, which stem from an acute sense of critical historical consciousness, reveal a commitment to method that seeks to be more comprehensive and universal. However, over 40 years Lonergan's focus remains unchanged; his principal concern is unwavering. We can safely say that his life's work centered around the human subject and the exploration of the range and depth of that human subjectivity.

The purpose of this chapter is to present what Lonergan means by human subjectivity. According to Lonergan, the subject realizes itself in an ever-progressive, ever-surpassing grasp of the self through authentic self-transcendence. To put it succinctly: for Lonergan, the human subject cannot be understood apart from its intrinsic exigence to transcend present possibilities. To express it in yet another way, Lonergan espouses an anthropology which holds that we can speak of the human subject only in as much as we draw our understanding from the subject's intrinsic drive to self-transcendence without which humans cannot be human. The discussion here will focus on the empirical and philosophical aspects of self-transcendence. In chapter four, we will explore horizons and conversions through which Lonergan considers self-transcendence at the intellectual, moral and religious levels. Thus the later chapter will show how human self-transcendence has its source as well as its destiny in God.

1.2. Development of the notion of human subjectivity

We will begin with a few basic questions: What is being human, according to Lonergan? Is there a significant difference between Lonergan's notion of the subject in his earlier works and in later works? In order to answer these questions, we will have to look at some of Lonergan's key essays that were published after *Insight* and before *Method in Theology*. In this chapter we will also examine Lonergan's own intellectual journey and take up those philosophers, theologians, and psychologists who influenced him. We will also deal with the mistaken notion that Lonergan is best seen as a Neo-Thomist or a Transcendental Thomist, whereby it is understood that his philosophical and theological heritage is to be seen predominantly in that light. This needs to be addressed because Lonergan's intellectual heritage can be traced both to Plato/Augustine/Newman as well as to Aristotle/Thomas. If this were not made clear, Lonergan's notion of subject would be equally difficult to understand.

Next, we will explore Lonergan's notion of the subject as self-transcendent, which will naturally lead us to the discussion of the subject's intentionality and consciousness. It is hardly possible to understand intentionality and consciousness apart from what Lonergan terms the subject's operation. This discussion will raise the question of what occurs as the subject moves from level to level of consciousness and intentionality. The answer lies in the subject achieving cognitive, affective, moral, and religious self-transcendence. Lonergan's notion of the subject would be incomplete without a detailed exposition of horizons and conversions. Our goal here will be to summarize briefly why horizons and conversions are crucial to understanding Lonergan's notion of the subject as self-transcendent. The subject operates, both at the level of intentionality and consciousness, in the world of meanings. Essentially, the subject seeks meaning through attempting to reflect on questions that lead to deeper questions. It is through this process that the subject achieves higher levels of transcendence, whether at the cognitive, affective, moral, or religious levels. For Lonergan, the horizon connotes the world of meaning from which the subject operates. When there is a radical shift in horizon there results a conversion. This conversion may occur in the cognitive, affective, moral or the religious realm. These conversions are the subject's realization of self-transcendence. A more in-depth treatment of horizon and conversions will follow in Chapter IV.

What is being human according to Lonergan? As we have pointed out earlier, Lonergan's work spans a period of over four decades. Hence the question: was there a consistency in how Lonergan understood what it is to be human? In his first major work *Insight*, Lonergan attempts to understand the human subject through a study of human understanding. Though the human subject we find in *Insight* is more than just an experiencing, inquiring, and judging subject, it must also be pointed out that there is a heavy emphasis on the subject as a cognitive agent. While Lonergan uses Aristotelian/Thomistic philosophical terms to speak of the human subject as knower, the subject is not presented as an immutable essence informed by a substantial form or merely as a combination of act and potency. Lonergan's notion of the subject in his earlier writings is constrained by his philosophical frame of reference. Though Lonergan was already conversant with existentialism and phenomenology, the influence of these philosophies is not altogether overt in this early work. When we read Lonergan's later works, especially the *Collection* and his lectures given in the years preceding the publication of *Method in Theology*, we are aware of a development in Lonergan's notion of the subject. Frederick Crowe writes, "One has to study *Verbum, Insight, Method,* and the papers of *A Third Collection* to realize the continually expanding dimensions of his thinking."[50]

In *Method in Theology*, written almost two decades after *Insight*, Lonergan presents a far clearer notion of the human subject. The earlier work explores understanding and the later work attempts to present a method for theology. Neither of them was intended to work out Lonergan's notion of the subject. However, neither human understanding nor method in theology can be achieved without the subject who understands and who does theology. In *Method in Theology*, Lonergan expands *Insight*'s predominantly cognitive notion of the subject to be multi-faceted and holistic. By this I mean that in *Insight* Lonergan's notion of the subject was shaped by the enterprise of understanding understanding and Lonergan appears to present the subject principally as knower. Hence, Lonergan's subject in *Insight* is less fully developed. In *Method in Theology*, Lonergan presents the human subject as cognitive, affective, moral, and religious. In each of these dimensions, the subject is dynamic and evolving. In fact, it is only in transcending one's present understanding and experience of the self that a subject becomes more and more authentically him/herself. In other words, the human subject realizes itself only through authentic self-transcendence.

Lonergan attained a certain sense of clarity in his notion of the human subject in the years that followed his magnum opus, *Insight*. In an attempt to explain and clarify that seminal work, Lonergan delivered a series of lectures in Halifax in 1958. These lectures were later published under the title, *Understanding and Being*. However, these lectures were intended only as an elaboration of what he had written in *Insight*, and they show little if any development. At the same time, these lectures foreground the subject, albeit, subject as knower and emphasize the dynamism of self-appropriation.

2. PHILOSOPHICAL INFLUENCES

In order to understand better the development of Lonergan's notion of human subjectivity and its range and depth, it would be necessary to dwell on Lonergan's own intellectual journey, which is intricately linked to the major influences on his thought. While keeping in mind that his earliest and most formative influences were those of the two traditions mentioned earlier,

Plato/Augustine/Newman and Aristotle/Thomas, we can now turn to philosophers, theologians, psychologists, and phenomenologists, who significantly influenced Lonergan's notion of the subject. To this task, we will now turn.

Lonergan's writings, while reflecting the philosophical tradition that shaped him, reveal "his equally profound commitment to transpose and to broaden the received traditions in the light of the turn to the human subject characteristic of modern thought."[51] Lonergan was devoted to studying the development of thought in modern philosophy. Hugo Meynell's *An Introduction to the Philosophy of Bernard Lonergan* makes it clear that the British empiricists, the German idealists and phenomenologists and existentialists serve as a background for the development of the thought of Lonergan. In what follows, I shall limit myself to the specific influences of empiricism, idealism, phenomenology, and existentialism on Lonergan's understanding of human subjectivity.

2.1 From the Greek Philosophers to Rene Descartes

From the time of the Greek philosophers, knowledge was seen as the result of observation of the objective universe. The concentration was on getting to the "essence" of reality. All knowledge revolved around the knowledge of the object in itself. Scholastic philosophy had perpetuated the objectification of knowledge by furthering the Greek notion of knowledge. Even the study of the human person in scholasticism, known as faculty psychology, was actually the study and rational analysis of the human person observed as another object for investigation. This approach would change once and for all with the revolutionary "turning to the subject" that Rene Descartes would initiate. Lonergan, like most contemporary philosophers and theologians, took the necessity of the "turn to the subject" very seriously. These general comments are not directly from Lonergan's writings. However, they are consistent with the way he spoke about Greek philosophy in his lectures and writings. A similar approach is followed in this section on the philosophical influences on Lonergan unless otherwise indicated.

Rene Descartes called into question the validity of knowledge that has no certainty. He proposed that knowledge and science should begin with firm and certain foundation. With his methodical doubt and his radical new beginning with "Cogito, ergo sum," Descartes is regarded as the one who called for a turn to the subject and radically changed the focus of scientific inquiry. Lonergan critiques Descartes and finds that his radical turn to the subject was not radical enough. Lonergan was convinced that one's epistemological and ontological edifice could not be built on mere thought process. It had to begin with the existential subject. The turn to the subject could not be partial, relegated to thought process alone. It must include the totality of the human person.

2.2. British Empiricists

Lonergan would begin, not from thought, but from an analysis of understanding. One might ask, if Lonergan begins with an analysis of understanding, how is he different from the British empiricists, Locke, Berkeley, and Hume, who also built up their epistemology and metaphysics from human understanding as their starting point? Though Lonergan and the classical empiricists begin at the same starting point, their conclusions are considerably divergent. Lonergan himself succinctly sums up the problem raised by the empiricists' position: "Are there really objects out there? Or, is *esse percipi*? Is it all in my perceiving?"[52] For Lonergan there is reality apart from one's perception. For Hume, knowledge consists of sense impressions which are put together by habit. All we know and can know comes to us only through our senses. There is no knowing beyond the senses or a complex combination of the senses.[53] For Lonergan, the senses provide us with only the raw data, which the subject experiences. The senses do not provide insight that is essential for understanding, judging, and deciding. Senses provide us with scattered pieces of sensory data. It is the subject who grasps the intelligible unity in those scraps of data and affirms that that intelligible unity is true or false by renewed appeals to data.[54] For example, contemporary science agrees that reality is made of invisible sub-atomic particles and that, even for science, reality is not just observed sense-reality.

2.3. Immanuel Kant

Lonergan was equally suspicious of the rationalism of Spinoza and Leibniz, who held that one could deduce everything from one's reason. Spinoza and Leibniz had developed the ideal of pure reason, which was systematically presented by Wolff. Immanuel Kant attacked "the ideal of pure reason"[55] in his *Critique of Pure Reason.* Lonergan agreed with Kant to the extent that we cannot deduce all knowledge from reason alone. In Lonergan's own view Kant's *Critique of Pure Reason* was "an attack upon types of philosophy that are deductivisitic in the Spinozaistic fashion."[56] Where did Lonergan part ways with Kant? Lonergan extended the same critique of pure reason to practical reason as well, but he laid bare the fallacy that we can come to all knowledge with the aid of practical reason. Lonergan's critique was more radical than that of Kant.

Lonergan himself addresses Kant in *Insight, Understanding and Being, Method in Theology* and in several other places.[57] What he said in Halifax Lecture 7 in the context of addressing the problem of objectivity in knowledge is probably the most succinct explanation of Lonergan's position. In order to make his position clear, he discusses the positions of Marechal[58] and de Tonquedec.[59] Both Marechal and de Tonquedec were critics of Kant's theory of knowledge, but in quite a contrasting manner. Lonergan holds that his position is different from that of Kant, as well as from those of Marechal and de Tonquedec as the following citation will clearly illustrate:

> Different answers here will determine different criticisms of Kant. Thus de Tonquedec holds that what is wrong with Kant is his ideal of pure reason and the categories of understanding; Kant should be content with intuition, and put more stress on intuition and not enough on judgment. Marechal, however, criticizes Kant for putting too much stress on intuition and not enough on judgment. My own position is that for Kant you have

knowing when intuition operates in such a way that you have concepts. But he does not recognize judgment and grasp of the unconditioned; he does not make the unconditioned a key point. The fundamental opposition is illustrated by Kant's position, and it is here that the basic issue comes to light. Kant's judgment that in knowledge we reach only phenomena is coherent if judgment is basic. That is, he can assert that this particular judgment is true and make it fundamental if the truth of judgment is fundamental. But, for Kant, judgment is not fundamental. Consequently, Kant's position does not square with his theory.[60]

2.4. Georg Hegel

Lonergan was also influenced by Hegel. In Lonergan's view, the discussion Kant had initiated by challenging a particular philosophic ideal, that of pure reason, was intensified and broadened by Hegel's challenge that any philosophical ideal must be made explicit. Lonergan recognized the validity of Hegel's challenge. Hegelian dialectics did play a role in Lonergan's theory of understanding as he presents it in *Insight* and in his whole approach to method, as is evident in his *Method in Theology*. David Tracy points out how "For Lonergan, then, the Hegelian dialectic included a recognition of the need to explicate all implicitly operative scientific and philosophic ideals. Moreover, the six central terms in Hegelian dialectic (implicit->explicit; abstract->alien; mediation->reconciliation) bespeak the presence of that recognition."[61]

However, there is a major difference between Hegel and Lonergan in the way each regards knowledge. For Hegel any philosophic or scientific knowledge that tries to explicitate an implicit ideal necessarily involves an ever-increasing abstraction of that ideal. From the beginning, we are doomed to abstraction and more abstraction, but abstraction is inevitably incapable of expressing reality.[62] Consequently, we are indubitably alienated from reality. For Lonergan, knowledge is not mere abstraction. The answer, for Lonergan, resides in the knower, the subject who knows. In the Halifax lectures, Lonergan says, "The difficulty is this: The pursuit of knowledge, the pursuit of a science, the

pursuit of a philosophy, is the pursuit of something that you don't know yet --
otherwise you would not be pursuing it -- and to account for that you have to
appeal to some sort of ideal."[63] He goes on to say that we have tendencies in us,
such as wonder, wanting to understand, wanting to understand things correctly
that have moved us from less adequate models of science to more adequate
formulations of the ideal. He lists the progression from the Aristotelian idea of
science through the Galilean idea of science, Newtonian science to the Einsteinian
idea of science, with the states and probabilities of quantum mechanics. In the
Hegelian framework, we are confined to the merely abstract. Lonergan's solution
is to root understanding in self-appropriation, which we shall deal with later in
greater detail.

2.5. Soren Kierkegaard

Another philosophical interlocutor who provided focus for Lonergan's
thinking was Soren Kierkegaard. Lonergan referred to the father of existentialism
often in his lectures and writings. Lonergan points out that Kierkegaard's
fundamental question, "Am I a Christian?" could be transposed in modern
existentialism as "Am I a man [sic]?" Kierkegaard's concern with moral and
religious values pose some significant questions to the Hegelian system.
However, Lonergan considers Kierkegaard to have not moved far enough to
explore the fundamental question, 'Am I a man/a human?' Although Kierkegaard
raised issues that helped to break out of a static notion of what it means to be
human, as Lonergan puts it, Kierkegaard "is concerned with the fact that he is the
realization, or he *should be* the realization, of some 'what ought to be'; that is one
way of putting it. It is a concern with existing, not in the scholastic sense of what
de facto is, but in the deontological, normative sense."[64] For Lonergan it is not
enough to move from a static to a dynamic, developmental view of what it is to be
human. He contends that "Kierkegaard is very much concerned with the states of
the individual in his development."[65] Existence in the deontological, normative
sense or as the realization of 'what ought to be' is found wanting in Lonergan's
view of Kierkegaard. The dynamism of being human must be seen in the context

of human exigence. Fundamental to Lonergan's notion of the human subject is intentionality. He himself writes how his notion of the human person is distinct from that of Aristotle:

> While Aristotelian psychology is not without profound insight into human sensibility and intelligence, still its basic concepts are derived not from intentional consciousness but from metaphysics. Thus "soul" does not mean "subject" but "the first act of an organic body" whether of a plant, an animal or a man. Similarly, the notion of "object" is not derived from a consideration of intentional acts; on the contrary, just as potencies are to be conceived by considering their acts, so acts are to be conceived by considering their objects, i.e. their efficient or final causes...Matter is pure potency. Movement is incomplete act, the act of what is in pure potency.[66]

There is a tendency in the human that far surpasses the actual, operative subject. The human subject cannot be understood only in terms of the operative subject. There is an intentionality that is not encompassed by the actual subject. In terms of potency and act, the act does not include the potency and yet is present within the agent. The human subject is self-transcendent. Any notion of the human subject that is not cognizant of self-transcendence is inadequate in Lonergan's view.

2.6. Edmund Husserl

Lonergan's subject as the knower was directly shaped by his study of phenomenology. Lonergan often referred to Husserl, and more especially to Heidegger. In Lecture 2 of his Halifax series, he makes explicit mention of the meeting of Phenomenologists at Louvain in 1951. Lonergan's intentionality analysis and horizon analysis show direct influence from phenomenology, particularly that of Husserl. When Lonergan writes, "In a word, phenomenology brackets reality to study acts in their intentionality,"[67] it seems as if this is what Lonergan's theory of knowledge is all about. Of course, intentionality and conscious operations are crucial to Lonergan's theory of knowledge and his understanding of the human subject. However, intentionality for Lonergan is firmly rooted in that one single pulsating thrust he terms 'self-transcendence'. Divorced from the subject as self-transcendent, intentionality has no place in Lonergan's thought.

3. PSYCHOLOGICAL INFLUENCES

Lonergan's understanding of the human subject was fashioned not only by his study of philosophy. He was keenly affected by his deep interest in psychology. His reading of psychologists like Sullivan is evident even in *Insight.* He makes several references to Sigmund Freud, Carl Jung, Alfred Adler, Ludwig Binswanger and Carl Rogers in his *Method in Theology*. Moreover, Lonergan himself acknowledged an indebtedness to Jean Piaget for the levels of consciousness an idea that is crucial in his understanding of the human person. It will benefit us in the context of this study to cite what Lonergan wrote about psychology and the development of the subject in the essay "A Post-Hegelian Philosophy of Religion":

> Beyond dreams, there is the daytime unfolding of this process that has been studied from different viewpoints by Jean Piaget, Erik Erikson, and Lawrence Kohlberg. Piaget examined operational development and placed its keys in a repeated *decentering* that keeps shifting the center of the subject's activity from himself to his ever enlarging universe. Erikson's approach is from depth psychology and his eight developmental stages are successive cumulative shifts in what one's *identity* becomes. Kohlberg, finally, attends to morals, distinguishes preconventional, conventional, and post-conventional morality, divides each into two stages, and reveals defects of each earlier stage as compared with its successor. It happens, however, that the ideas of all three writers have been brought in a unitary view in terms of self-transcendence.[68]

4. SUBJECT AS SUBJECT

We will now turn to a significant lecture that Lonergan delivered at Marquette University that adds clarity to his understanding of the human subject. The lecture was entitled "The Subject," in which Lonergan gave a lucid presentation of his understanding of the existential subject by contrasting it with other notions of the subject that leave much to be desired. In the present section, I shall attempt to highlight the main thrust of Lonergan's argument in this lecture.[69] He grants that much of the credit for "the turning to the subject" in contemporary philosophy may be traced to the influence of Hegel, Kierkegaard, Nietzsche, Heidegger, and Buber. He avers that this "turning to the subject" only indicates a previous period of neglect and enumerates several causes for it in the past.

4.1. The Neglected Subject

One source of neglect of the subject can be traced to an exaggerated insistence on the objectivity of truth, which was so one-sided as to leave subjects and their needs out of account. Theologians fell victim to the same kind of one-sidedness of objectivity that "they seem to have thought of truth as so objective as to get along without minds."[70] For Lonergan, it is the subject who arrives at the truth. However, "once truth is attained, one is beyond the subject and one has reached a realm that is non-spatial, atemporal, impersonal."[71] He insists that "intentionally it [objectivity of truth] is independent of the subject, but ontologically it resides only in the subject: *veritas formaliter est in solo iudicio*."[72] The subject and the objectivity of truth must be brought to proper balance.

A second source of neglect of the subject is connected in some way with the Aristotelian notion of science, traces of which we can find in the rationalist idea of pure reason. When science and, for that matter, philosophy derive conclusions necessarily from premises that are self-evident, then the subject has no place in arriving at the conclusion. Everything is self-evident; everything is demonstrable. Then the subject is dispensable. In this scheme of things, there is no place for open-mindedness, striving, perseverance or intellectual conversion.

Still another source of neglect of the subject is linked to the metaphysical account of the soul. Plants and animals are said to have souls. The problem was that the study of the soul was totally objective. There was no distinction between the souls of the lower forms and of the human. There was one method that was used to study all. Lonergan insists that the souls of each order are essentially different.

> To discern these differences, we must turn from the soul to its potencies, habits, acts, and objects. Through the objects we know the acts, through the acts we know the habits, through the habits we know the potencies, and through the potencies we know the essence of the soul.[73]

Lonergan, then, points out the most crucial difference in studying the subject: the human person is the agent who studies him/herself inasmuch as one is conscious. "It prescinds from the soul, its essence, its potencies, its habits, for none of these are given in consciousness. It attends to operations and to their center and source which is the self."[74] Lonergan reiterates that "subject and soul, then, are two quite different topics. To know one does not exclude the other in any way. But it very easily happens that the study of the soul leaves one with the feeling that one has no need to study the subject and, to that extent, leads to a neglect of the subject."[75]

4.2. The Truncated Subject

There are others who, according to Lonergan, do not neglect the subject, but nevertheless truncate it. Whether it be empiricists, who concede only to the possibility of what is known through the senses, or be it behaviorists who do not admit anything beyond the mechanistic maneuverings, allowing for nothing like the inner workings of the subject, or be it logical positivists, who restrict the possibility of knowing only to sensible data or mathematics, logic, or be it pragmatists who are oriented only to action and results, all of them inevitably end in an oversight of insight. "It is only by close attention to the data of consciousness that one can discover insights, acts of understanding with the triple role of responding to inquiry, grasping the intelligible form in sensible representations, and grounding the formation of concepts."[76] Lonergan points out that the neglected subject often leads to the truncated subject, "to the subject that does not know himself and so unduly impoverishes his account of human knowledge. He condemns himself to an anti-historical mobilism, to an excessively jejune conjunction between abstract concepts and sensible presentations, and to ignorance of the proleptic and utterly concrete character of the notion of being."[77] Empiricists, behaviorists, logical positivists, and pragmatists do not admit the validity of data of consciousness and consequently leave no possibility for a dynamic, vibrant, existential subject.

4.3. The Immanentist Subject

Lonergan here refers to and attacks the Kantian subject, summarizing the Kantian argument:

> In this argument the effective distinction is between immediate and mediate relations of cognitional activities to objects. Judgment is only a mediate knowledge of activities to objects, a representation of a representation. Reason is never related right up to objects but only to understanding and, through understanding, to the empirical use of reason itself. Since our only cognitional activity immediately related to objects is intuition, it follows that the value of our judgments and our reasoning can be no more than the value of our intuitions. But our only intuitions are sensitive; sensitive intuitions reveal not being but phenomena; and so our judgments and reasoning are confined to a merely phenomenal world.[78]

Lonergan distinguishes between three kinds of objectivity: there is an experiential objectivity that is found in the data of the senses and the data of consciousness; then, there is an objectivity arrived at by the exigencies of human intelligence and human reasonableness which aid us in formulating logic and methodologies; and finally, there is an absolute type of objectivity that we employ when we judge. Lonergan insists that an object is something that one looks at, while objectivity is a matter of seeing all that is there and nothing that is not there. He speaks of "picture-thinking." In picture-thinking, one looks at the object, the whole of what is presented to the subject. It is sensitive intuition and as such is related immediately to the object.

4.4. The Existential Subject

The subject is not merely the one who is the knower, the one who experiences, understands, and judges. The subject is also the one who is the doer, the one who deliberates, evaluates, chooses and acts. While the world of objects is certainly affected and modified, the subject is affected even more. The human subject is a doer endowed with freedom and responsibility. It is this freedom and responsibility that makes it possible for moral action and formation of character. It is the exercise of freedom and responsibility that shapes the subject and thus the subject creates his/her own destiny. This notion of the subject, according to Lonergan, had been overlooked by philosophies that spoke of the person in terms of intellect and will or speculative and practical intellect. Lonergan draws attention to the fact that "while the reflective, self-constitutive element in moral living has been known from ancient times, still it was not coupled with the notion of the subject to draw attention to him in his key role of making himself what he is to be."[79]

In a later section, when we elaborate on the levels of consciousness, we will have a more in-depth understanding of what Lonergan means by the existential subject. However, our discussion contrasting Lonergan's subject from those of the empiricists, the rationalists, the idealists, and the Kantian and the Hegelian views of the subject clarified for us some preliminary notion of the existential subject. Lonergan's explication of the neglected subject, the truncated subject, and the immanentist subject gave a sharper focus to the existential subject.

5. SUBJECT AS CONSCIOUS

Thus far, we have explored Lonergan's notion of the subject, the vibrant, existential subject. We clarified who the subject is for Lonergan by critically examining how Lonergan's knower differs from those of the empiricists, the rationalists, and the idealists. Lonergan's treatment of the neglected subject, the truncated subject, the immanentist subject, and the alienated subject was beneficial to us in focusing our understanding of who Lonergan's existential subject is. This treatment of the subject should not lead us to regard the subject as a mere agent of knowledge, as an agent who goes through a set of motions or operations to achieve some objective knowledge. In order to avoid this misunderstanding, we need to highlight that Lonergan always holds the subject to be a conscious subject, a subject who not only knows but who knows that s/he knows. We cannot disregard the awareness of the subject in the act of knowing, without running the risk of undermining the depth and the wealth of the existential subject. When we speak of the subject-as-subject, we are in fact speaking of the subject-as-conscious.

How is the subject conscious? How does the subject know that s/he knows? The human subject interacts with objects and the world around her. S/he attempts to grasp the object as s/he encounters it. As we have already explained, what the subject encounters are the sensations associated with the object. First, it is a sense response. But, it does not stop there. Human knowledge is not merely a cumulative sense response as it was for the empiricists, nor is it something that is in the mind of the subject as an idea as it was for the rationalists, nor was it just the apprehension of the phenomena as it was for Kant. There is a real objectivity about the truth of the knowledge that the subject acquires. What the senses provide us are raw data – but without any organization or pattern. How does the subject know that it is he who knows? What makes it possible for him to be aware of his knowing?

5.1. Insight

Lonergan's breakthrough came early on in his first major work, *Insight*. As the title suggests, insight is central to understanding Lonergan. Hugo Meynell rightly points out that the term 'insight' is the clue. The data provided by our senses gives us only scraps of information which come to us at random, with no particular pattern. Experience furnishes us only uncoordinated scraps of data. It is the conscious subject that puts these bits of uncoordinated data into a pattern that has an intelligible unity. The central problem that empiricists faced was the bridging of the sense data and the intelligible unity in human knowledge. None of them had made this breakthrough.

Lonergan was able to make this discovery possible because he saw the human subject able to go beyond, to transcend the mere sense data and to be capable of bringing together all the scattered pieces of data into a coherent, orderly, and intelligible whole. Hume and Kant had, according to Lonergan, restricted the intelligibility of the observed world as residing in the human mind, with no possibility of inferring that it exists in reality itself prior to the imposition of that intelligible unity by the human mind in the act of understanding. Lonergan holds that through insight, the subject transcends the chasm that exists between the intelligent subject and the intelligible object. In fact, the intelligible unity of the observed reality is not a creation of the subject, rather the subject through insight arrives at the intelligible pattern that already resides in the object. Thus the subject postulates a theory from the experiential data of the observed reality. The subject does not accept its apprehension of reality arbitrarily. Understanding is further put to the test. The subject seeks to affirm the truth of what is experienced and understood by continually appealing to that data for verification or falsification of the theory. It is the conscious subject, who in each of the three stages of the process of human knowledge, experience, understanding, and judgment that makes knowledge happen. It is the subject who knows that he knows, who knows that he understands, and who knows he judges. The question is, how does the subject bring this about? Lonergan's simple answer is by "self-appropriation."

5.2. Self-Appropriation

Lonergan detects a contradiction in some of the philosophers of the nineteenth century, who started their epistemology with the existence of knowledge. He holds this to be contradictory, for a theory of knowledge cannot assume the existence of knowledge; it must first establish the existence of knowledge. In fact, this is Lonergan's explicit purpose in *Insight*. We have shown how Lonergan begins with the experience of sensory data, which comes to the subject in no particular pattern, which the subject, by insight, puts together into an orderly, coherent theory, and by judgment affirms the validity or falsity of that theory by constantly testing it against the data. Lonergan, thus establishes the existence and the validity of human knowledge. The big question is, how does the subject make this happen? According to Lonergan, the subject makes this happen by self-appropriation.

What is self-appropriation? As we shall elaborate in greater detail later, Lonergan notes that the subject is the agent of a basic pattern of operations. He lists these operations as: "seeing, hearing, touching, smelling, tasting, inquiring, imagining, understanding, conceiving, formulating, reflecting, marshalling, and weighing the evidence, judging, deliberating, evaluating, deciding, speaking, writing."[80] These operations are foundational for Lonergan's methodology and he refers to them constantly in his writings and even when he does not do so explicitly, he holds them in the background. The transcendental notions and the transcendental method he expounds are crucially linked to these operations. It is essential to reiterate the subject for Lonergan is far more than a grammatical construct. He writes, "The operator is subject not merely in the grammatical sense that he is denoted by a noun that is subject of the verbs that in the active voice refer to the operations. He is also subject in the psychological sense that he operates consciously. In fact, none of the operations in the list is to be performed in dreamless sleep or in a coma. Again whenever any of the operations are performed, the subject is aware of himself operating, present to himself operating, experiencing himself operating."

It is clear, we are dealing with a conscious subject. However, we must make a crucial distinction. The subject experiencing himself operating is not another operation among the other operations. The subject is conscious of himself as operating. Consciousness of oneself as the operator at all levels of operations is what self-appropriation is.

A further clarification can be obtained by addressing a related question: What exactly happens when one is trying to achieve self-appropriation? Lonergan himself asks this question in his Halifax lectures. He answers the question by distinguishing three modes of 'presence'. First, there is the way an object is present as in the case of a chair in a room. It does not require a conscious subject to acknowledge the presence of the object. Second, there is the way something or someone is present to a conscious subject. It means that there is the object present to a conscious subject. Finally, there is the way a subject is present to him/herself. In self-appropriation, we are dealing with the third mode or way of presence.[81] We need to be careful not to be misled into regarding self-appropriation as being synonymous with introspection. Introspection connotes only an inward inspection. This misconception rests on the mistaken analogy that all cognitional events are to be understood in the analogy of ocular vision. Introspection denotes taking a look at oneself. But, as Lonergan points out, "You cannot turn yourself inside out and take a look."[82] In achieving self-appropriation, the subject transcends the object he is attending to, to the subject who is attending.

Consciousness and self-appropriation are not to be regarded as a process of objectifying the content of consciousness. Self-appropriation is the process of consciousness itself. As Lonergan puts it,

> First of all, self-appropriation is advertence-- advertence to oneself as experiencing, understanding, and judging. Secondly, it is understanding oneself as experiencing, understanding, and judging. Thirdly, it is affirming oneself as experiencing, understanding, and judging. The analysis of knowledge, then yields three elements: experience, understanding, judging.[83]

It is evident that self-appropriation cannot be done vicariously. The subject becomes the subject "not by reading books or listening to lectures or analyzing language."[84] One has to achieve self-appropriation for oneself. No one can achieve it for another. There is a conscious possession of oneself as subject that is essential to understanding the existential subject. This conscious possession of oneself as subject is not static. It is dynamic, open, progressive and cumulative. As the existential subject achieves greater self-appropriation through the process of experiencing, understanding, and judging, she realizes a fuller awareness of the self. In fact, she becomes a fuller self. When we talk about self-appropriation through the process of experiencing, understanding, and judging, we are speaking primarily of the knowing subject. The existential subject is far more than the knowing subject. Consequently, Lonergan speaks of higher levels of self-appropriation as the subject decides, acts, and loves responsibly.

5.3. Levels of Consciousness and Intentionality

In *Insight*, Lonergan speaks of levels of consciousness, but he seems to be focusing predominantly on the cognitive dimension of consciousness. He admitted that there was not a clear delineation of the levels of deliberation and action, which go beyond the cognitive dimension. In 1968, Lonergan rectifies this absence in *The Subject*. When Lonergan showed the deficiencies of "older schemes" of the subject, he attempted to bring greater clarity to the understanding of the existential subject by indicating

> the new scheme of distinct but related levels of consciousness...For we are subjects, as it were, by degrees. At a lowest level, when unconscious in dreamless sleep or in a coma, we are merely potentially subjects. Next, we have a minimal degree of consciousness and subjectivity when we are the helpless subjects of our dreams. Thirdly, we become experiential subjects when we awake, when we become the subjects of lucid perception, imaginative projects, emotional and cognitive impulses, and bodily actions. Fourthly, the intelligent subject sublates the experiential, i.e., it retains, preserves, goes beyond, completes it, when we inquire about our experience, investigate, grow in understanding, express our inventions and discoveries. Fifthly, the rational subject sublates the intelligent and experiential subject, when we question our own understanding, check our formulations and expressions, ask whether we have got things right, marshal the evidence *pro* and *con*, judge this to be so and that not to be so.

Sixthly, finally, rational consciousness is sublated by rational self-consciousness, when we deliberate, evaluate, decide, act. Then there emerges human consciousness at its fullest. Then the existential subject exists and his character, his personal essence, is at stake.[85]

In subsequent years, Lonergan brought more depth and clarity to the various levels of consciousness, especially to the level of deliberation, and responsible action.

In *Method in Theology*, Lonergan speaks of "four successive, related, but qualitatively different levels,"[86] beyond the dream state where consciousness is mostly fragmentary and incoherent. These four levels he enumerates: 1. the empirical level, the level of sensing, perceiving, imagining, feeling, speaking and moving; 2. the intellectual level, the level of inquiring, coming to understand, expressing what we understand, working out the presuppositions and implications of our expressions; 3. the rational level, the level of reflecting, marshalling the evidence, passing judgment on truth or falsity; and 4. the responsible level, the level of deliberating about our course of action, evaluating it, deciding on it, and carrying it out in our lives.

5.4. Conscious Operations

According to Lonergan, at the various levels of consciousness, the subject is the agent of various operations. These operations are numerous. Throughout his life, Lonergan explored these operations. In *Insight*, as was pointed out earlier, the predominant emphasis was on the cognitive operations. However, in his later writings, Lonergan spoke of existential operations in greater detail. Lonergan enumerates these operations as experience, understanding, judging, deciding, acting, and loving. Lonergan himself expands on the various operations.

"Their operations are both conscious and intentional. But what is conscious, can be intended. To apply the operations as intentional to the operations as conscious is a fourfold matter of (1) experiencing one's experiencing, understanding, judging, and deciding, (2) understanding the unity and relations of one's experienced experiencing, understanding, judging, deciding, (3) affirming the reality of one's experienced and understood experiencing, understanding, judging, deciding, and (4) deciding to operate in accord with the norms immanent in the spontaneous relatedness of one's experienced, understood, affirmed experiencing, understanding and judging, and deciding."[87]

Each of these operations builds on the previous and sublates[88] them. According to Lonergan, sublation means the subject has progressed from the lower operation to the higher without having lost what the subject had acquired in the previous operation. In other words, the subject who understands has not lost what s/he had experienced, but builds on that experience. In fact, experience is essential to understanding. We can clearly see here the influence of Jean Piaget's cognitive developmental theory.

6. SUBJECT AS SELF-TRANSCENDENT

As has been explained, it is clear that Lonergan's enterprise was to focus on human understanding. To be more precise, it was to understand understanding. From the very beginning, Lonergan was convinced that in order to understand understanding, it was necessary to focus on the subject because it is the human subject who knows. It was his contention that the reason why many philosophies do not answer the questions of epistemology adequately is because they do not begin with the human subject, but rather with a truncated account of the human subject which takes what is only a part to be the whole. Lonergan finds his answer to the objectivity of human knowledge in the human subject. It is the subject, who, through self-appropriation, makes sense of reality. It is the subject, who understands, experiences and judges. It is the ability to transcend the confines of one's own limitedness and to reach beyond oneself that makes objective human knowledge possible.

The first and most important part of self-appropriation, as we have noted, is insight. This is the ability of the subject not to be a mere observer, an on-looker, but to be the one who transcends one's sensual experience. It means that raw data, which meets the subject through the senses, does not remain a collection of unrelated pieces of information. Through insight, the subject perceives the unity and coherence of the sensual data. Insight is, indeed, the first instance of self-transcendence of the human subject. The human subject is not limited to the realm of insights alone. We have also shown how Lonergan's subject is not confined by the limits of unconscious moments of self-transcendence. The human knower is a knower who knows that he knows. In other words, the human subject is a conscious subject. The knowing subject transcends the confines of the perceived world to the world that exists outside the subject. The act of knowing and understanding clearly brings out the self-transcendence of the subject.

6.1. Levels of Consciousness and Self-transcendence

We have dealt at length with consciousness and intentionality and its ramifications in the various levels of operation. We need to revisit those important notions once again in order to draw out some significant implications for the subject's self-transcendence.

Lonergan distinguishes various levels of consciousness and intentionality. Initially, as evidenced in *Insight*, Lonergan focused primarily, though not exclusively, on the cognitive levels. However, by the time he wrote *Method in Theology*, he presented a more comprehensive view. There is a dream state of consciousness and intentionality, which Lonergan points out, are normally fragmentary and incoherent. However, in the waking state, human consciousness and intentionality "take on a different hue to expand on four successive, related, but qualitatively different levels."[89] The precise and concise descriptions of these levels are best presented in Lonergan's own words:

> There is the *empirical* level on which we sense, perceive, imagine, feel, speak, and move. There is an intellectual level on which we inquire, come to understand, express what we have understood, and work out the presuppositions and implications of our expression. There is the rational level on which we reflect, marshal the evidence, pass judgment on the truth or falsity, certainty or probability, of a statement. There is the

responsible level on which we are concerned with ourselves, our own operations, our goals, and so deliberate about possible courses of action, evaluate them, decide, and carry out our decisions.[90]

Lonergan sees the progressive movement and expansion into the various levels as decisively different levels of consciousness and intentionality, differing from the other levels and having within each level many operations, which involve further differences.

Our consciousness expands in a new dimension when from mere experiencing we turn to the effort to understand what we have experienced. A third dimension of rationality emerges when the content of our acts of understanding is regarded as, of itself, a mere bright idea and we endeavor to settle what really is so. A fourth dimension comes to the fore when judgment on the facts is followed by deliberation on what we are to do about them.[91]

Movements from one level to another are break-throughs from a lower level to a higher level that is substantially progressive and qualitatively different. They are moments of self-transcendence. In reaching and operating at the intellectual level, the human subject has moved far beyond the confines of the empirical level. The human subject has transcended its own awareness and consciousness of self at the empirical level. Sense perceptions and the data collection have been transcended. At the intellectual level, the subject is not simply acquiring data, but organizing data into intelligible wholes. The subject has pushed consciousness and operations to a plane beyond the empirical level.

The same reality of self-transcendence is integral to the movement from the intellectual level to the rational level and from the rational level to the responsible level. While at the intellectual level, the subject is capable of organizing data into intelligible wholes; it is incapable of reflection and critical rationality. However, in breaking through to the rational level, the subject is capable of rational analysis and critical judgment that makes it possible to commit itself to truth and certitude. At this stage, however, the subject is not making responsible decisions. It is only in the responsible level that the subject is drawn by values and is required to use its freedom to become a fuller human person.

What has become clear is that the human subject, through its unfolding movement from lower to higher levels of consciousness, demonstrates that it transcends itself progressively and becomes itself more and more fully. Lonergan puts it this way, "On all four levels, we are aware of ourselves but, as we mount from level to level, it is a fuller self of which we are aware and the awareness itself is different."[92]

6.2. Levels of intentionality and self-transcendence

When Lonergan talks about the levels of consciousness and intentionality, there is a tendency to concentrate on the levels of consciousness and ignore the levels of intentionality. In connection with this study, the levels of intentionality are as important as the levels of consciousness. The levels of consciousness deal with what we experience, understand, decide, and act reflectively; they are confined to the empirical realm. On the other hand, intentionality is the tendency, the potency to forge ahead. From the realm of the known we push forward into the realms of the unknown.[93] Thus self-transcendence becomes intricately linked to intentionality. This is not to say that the conscious operations are not self-transcending, but rather they are two different operations that help the subject actualize one's self-transcendence. Lonergan seems to concentrate on the levels of consciousness more often than on the levels of intentionality. However, he is clear in stating that the levels of consciousness and intentionality are not to be confused as being identical. Lonergan writes,

> As different operations yield qualitatively different modes of being conscious subjects, so too they yield qualitatively different modes of intending. The intending of our senses is an attending; it normally is selective but not creative. The intending of our imagination may be representative or creative. What is grasped in insight, is neither an actually given datum of sense nor a creation of the imagination but an intelligible organization that may or may not be relevant to data.[94]

We have shown how conscious and intentional operations are crucial o our understanding of the subject's self-transcendence. It is in each level of operation of the subject as conscious and as intentional that self-transcendence is actualized and realized. When we enter into the discussion of self-transcendence that is effected through conversion we will have a fuller picture of what we have so far spoken about self-transcendence.

Lonergan then goes on to state that the most fundamental difference in the modes of intending lies between the categorical and the transcendental. Categories are determinations; they have a limited denotation. They vary with cultural variations. Transcendentals are comprehensive in connotation, unrestricted in denotation, invariant over cultural change. In Lonergan's words,

> While categories are needed to put determinate questions and give determinate answers, the transcendentals are contained in questions prior to the answers. They are the radical intending that moves us from ignorance to knowledge. They are a *a priori* because they go beyond what we know to seek what we do not know yet. They are unrestricted because answers are never complete and so only give rise to still further questions. They are comprehensive because they intend the unknown whole or totality of which our answers reveal only part. So intelligence takes us beyond experiencing to ask what and why and how and what for. Reasonableness takes us beyond the answers of intelligence to ask whether the answers are true and whether what they mean really is so. Responsibility goes beyond fact and desire and possibility to discern between what truly is good and what only apparently is good.[95]

It can never be overstated that basic to the various levels of consciousness and intentionality is the single dynamism that pushes the subject from the lower levels to the higher. This is what Lonergan constantly speaks about when he talks of the single thrust that unifies the human subject. Indeed, it is to this that he keeps returning in all his works--the drive to transcendence that is intrinsic to being human. This self-transcendence is not another quality or aspect of the subject; it is the subject. It is the subject who brings about the higher integration. It is the subject who is self-transcendent.

6.3. Subject and Meaning

In his earlier writings, Lonergan talked about insight and about understanding. However, during the years prior to his *Method in Theology*, Lonergan's own intellectual journey brought him to focus his attention on meaning and its importance to the human enterprise. It must, however, be noted that Lonergan was not rejecting what he had done in his earlier phase. He did not minimize the importance of insight and understanding. He always considered *Insight* as the seminal work and his subsequent writings as stemming from it and being rooted in it. In Lonergan's own intellectual development, this expansion was inevitable. "Lonergan's involvement in historical consciousness forced him to shift his interest from an almost exclusive concern with scientific intelligibility to study the multidimensional character of meaning."[96] Lonergan expanded on the transcendental method that he had used in *Insight*, but he himself admitted on several occasions that he had somewhat restricted himself to the cognitive domain in his earlier work and wanted to look effectively at the whole of the human enterprise. In this expansion, he was convinced that meaning had to play a central role. Lonergan believed that "different exigencies give rise to different modes of conscious and intentional operation, and different modes of such operation give rise to different realms of meaning."[97] This is also our key to understanding how Lonergan grasped meaning as intimately linked to self-transcendence. This will be our present task: to explore what is meaning in Lonergan's thinking, how he linked meaning and the human subject, and how meaning is tied to self-transcendence in the human subject.

Lonergan devotes an entire chapter in his *Method in Theology* to "Meaning" and yet he does not gives us a succinct definition of what meaning is. As David Tracy points out, "Meaning is a paradoxical term. It may not be tied down to some universal, essential definition so beloved to the classical mind nor may its endlessly elusive character be exhausted in scientific meaning alone."[98]

However, for Lonergan, the notion of meaning is intricately linked to Piaget's findings in developmental psychology. Lonergan agrees with Piaget that an infant's world is one of immediacy: "The world of the infant is no bigger than the nursery. It is the world of what is felt, touched, grasped, sucked, seen, heard. It is a world of immediate experience, of the given as given, of image and affect without any perceptible intrusion from insight or concept, reflection or judgment or deliberation or choice. It is the world of pleasure and pain, hunger and thirst, food and drink, rage and satisfaction and sleep."[99] The infant interacts directly with the world. However, as the child begins to develop, it is taken out of the world of immediacy and placed in the adult's world, which is a world mediated by meaning. With the development of language, the child transcends the world of immediacy, the world of the present to the far wider world that is already past or what is not yet in the future. As Lonergan puts it, "For words denote not only what is present but also what is absent or past or future, not only what is factual but also the possible, the ideal, the normative."[100] The child has moved out of the confines of the world of immediacy and the self has transcended to worlds that are not only here and now, but into the realm of seemingly endless possibilities.

How the subject achieves self-transcendence through the search for meaning is clearly brought out by Lonergan in the following passage:

> This larger world, mediated by meaning, does not lie within anyone's immediate experience. It is not even the sum, the integral, of the totality of all the worlds of immediate experience. For meaning is an act that does not merely repeat but goes beyond experiencing. For what is meant, is what is intended in questioning and is determined not only by experience but also by understanding and, commonly, by judgment as well. This addition of understanding and judgment is what makes possible the world mediated by meaning, what gives it its structure and unity, what arranges it in an orderly whole of almost endless differences partly known and familiar, partly in a surrounding penumbra of things we know about but have never examined or explored, partly an unmeasured region of what we do not know at all.[101]

To understand Lonergan's notion of meaning, David Tracy uses the two basic methods of approach that Lonergan himself had used in *Insight*: the descriptive and the analytic. In Tracy's own words, "From a descriptive standpoint, one may enumerate the realities which proceed from meaning, which are in fact constituted by meaning. From an analytic viewpoint, one may work out the constituents of meaning by determining the acts and structures in and through which meanings emerge. Both procedures obviously presuppose meaning and use it."[102] Both procedures lead us to understand what a crucial part meaning played in Lonergan's notion of the subject as self-transcendent.

From the descriptive approach we come to understand the multiple nature of meaning and the importance of meaning. From this standpoint, meaning is constitutive. In Lonergan's thinking, the human subject from the dream state to the various stages of conscious state is "fundamentally a creature and creator of that aspect of being called meaning--his arts, symbols, literatures, history, natural and human sciences, families, states, philosophies, religions and theologies. For though meaning be not the sole constituent of human potentiality, it is the field in which arise good and evil, right and wrong, truth and error, grace and sin, salvation and damnation."[103] Meaning is constitutive "of all our projects, of our endless questions, of our acts and developing habits of understanding, of our explanations of possibility in mathematics or logic or fiction, of our doubts, affirmations and negations, our beliefs and opinions, convictions and certitudes."[104] Meaning is what makes us who we are and enables us to understand who we are. It is through meaning that we move beyond our present actuality and transcend our limitedness to worlds and horizons that are presently beyond our reach. It is the subject's ability to question and seek meaning that makes it possible to transcend the lower levels of consciousness and intentionality to the higher levels[105] and as we shall see, it is the same ability to question and seek meaning that renders it possible to broaden our horizon and bring about conversion in the intellectual, moral, and religious planes.

Lonergan presents multiple dimensions and expressions of meaning, most of which are significant in respect to the current discussion. David Tracy lists seven such expressions in Lonergan's thought: intersubjective meaning, incarnate meaning, symbolic meaning, aesthetic meaning, everyday meaning, literary communication of meaning, and technical communication of meaning.

6.4. Intersubjectivity of Meaning

Lonergan speaks of the intersubjectivity of meaning that is prior to interpersonal relationship. In terms reminiscent of Martin Buber, Lonergan writes, "Prior to the 'we' that results from the mutual love of an 'I' and a 'thou', there is the earlier 'we' that precedes the distinction of subjects and survives its oblivion....It is as if 'we' were members of one another prior to our distinctions of each from the others."[106] Lonergan uses what he calls "a phenomenology of a smile" to illustrate the intersubjective nature of meaning. "A smile does have a meaning. It is not just a certain combination of movements of lips, facial muscles, and eyes. It is a combination with a meaning. Because that meaning is different from the meaning of a frown, a scowl, a stare, a glare, a snicker, a laugh, it is named a smile."[107] We do not learn to smile as we learn to walk or talk, nor do we learn the meaning of smiling as we learn the meaning of words. There is a sense of transcending oneself through the smile. We reach beyond ourselves to another. The intersubjective nature of meaning makes this possible.

Then there is the symbolic meaning. For Lonergan, it is "an image of a real or imaginary object that evokes a feeling or is evoked by a feeling."[108] Symbols are intricately and intimately connected with the construction of meaning that subjects are engaged in throughout their lives. In David Tracy's words, "Symbols are the primordial expression of that affectivity and aggressivity that relate us to our worlds of meaning."[109] The importance of symbols in the self-transcendent subject are elaborated on by Lonergan thus,

> One desires the good that is absent, hopes for the good that is sought, enjoys the good that is present; one fears the absent evil, becomes disheartened at its approach, sad in its presence. Again, feelings are related to one another through personal relationships: so love, gentleness, tenderness, intimacy, union go together; similarly, alienation, hatred,

violence, cruelty form a group; so too there are such sequences of offense, contumacy, judgment, punishment and again, offense, repentance, apology, forgiveness.... Finally, feelings are related to their subjects: they are the mass and momentum and power of his conscious living, the actuation of his affective capacities, dispositions, habits, the effective orientation of his being."[110]

7. CONCLUSION

In this chapter I have attempted to lay out Lonergan's notion of the subject. The phrase 'notion of the subject' seems to lack the dynamism that is intrinsic to the way Lonergan understands what it means to be human. For Lonergan, to be human means to be in a continuous, progressive movement of self-transcendence. To the extent that a person actualizes one's possibilities in authentic self-transcendence that person realizes the humanity that he or she is. We would do grave injustice to Lonergan if we limit his understanding of what it means to be human to what I have said in this chapter. Lonergan was a philosopher-theologian. As a theologian he probes the religious and spiritual dimensions of what it means to be human. Lonergan's discussions of horizons and conversions take us to the religious and spiritual dimensions of what it means to be human. As we turn our attention to this in chapter four, we will be building on what we have described in chapter two.

CHAPTER III
PERSON AS MEANING-MAKER

1. INTRODUCTION: KEGAN AND LONERGAN

In the previous chapter, we presented what being human meant for Lonergan. According to this philosopher-theologian, the human subject is in constant pursuit of transcendence, which the individual realizes by achieving an ever-greater grasp of the self through a heuristic process of discovering the unknown within oneself in the cognitive, affective, and the moral realms. In the present chapter, we shall explore Harvard psychologist, Robert Kegan's theory of human development. At the very outset, it must be stated that Kegan in presenting his theory is not explicitly attempting to articulate a specifically philosophical or theological theory about what it means to be human. However, the theory does offer us a concrete way of understanding what it means to be human by the continual thrust towards constructing meaning of one's present experiences and continually progressing to higher grasp of the self. Consequently, there is a fundamental concurrence in the way philosopher-theologian, Lonergan and psychologist, Kegan understand what it means to be human. In order to understand Kegan's theory, we will provide some salient background to his intellectual and psychological heritage. This will also give us a better understanding of the context for his theory. Then, we will proceed to present his stage theory of ego-development which he calls "The Evolving Self." As our task here is not intended to be evaluative but interpretative, we will limit our critique of Kegan's theory to a minimum.

2. KEGAN IN THE PIAGETIAN TRADITION

Kegan acknowledges that he comes in the line of Jean Piaget. To better understand Kegan's connection to Piaget we need to hear how Kegan sees himself in regard to Piaget. Sigmund Freud and Jean Piaget have made singular contributions to the study of the human person. They have profoundly revolutionized the way we regard ourselves. Their original contributions have inspired and influenced a host of other thinkers. Kegan is one such theorist greatly influenced by the genius of Piaget. Kegan considers himself indebted to Piaget even as Erik Erikson owed his theory to the original contributions of Freud. Kegan writes, "Erikson's genius was Sigmund Freud. Mine has been Jean Piaget."[111] Erikson's interest was in ego-development, so is Kegan's. Kegan admits, "What Erikson found himself led to through Freud is what it seems to me I have been led to in a new form by Piaget -- a highly elaborated surmise about the development of the ego."[112] Kegan's singular insight into Piaget has given birth to a very significant theory of ego-development.

Piaget's tradition has been referred to by various names. Kegan refers to Piaget's unique contribution as "constructivism." This label has been widely used in the field of education and does convey assimilation and accommodation that results in the construction of a new idea, development or stage, very similar to a child constructing his/her world. Piaget saw himself as a genetic epistemologist—he saw the embryogenetic development of a fetus to be the model of the development of all mental (human) faculties. As one of Piaget's collaborators has said, "The design is realized progressively, and the structures that are constructed, or the parts, the organs, that are constructed start to interact and are built by interaction with each other."[113] Piaget's tradition is often called 'structuralism.'[114]

Kegan, like Piaget is a structuralist. According to Hugh Rosen, "Structuralism is a method of analyzing and understanding phenomena rather than a dogma of content. The structuralist scans the surface manifestations of things or events and penetrates below these to grasp the underlying order and significance which form a meaningful pattern." [115] Kegan, like Piaget, observes and studies the human person and grasps the underlying order and significance, which form a meaningful pattern, which is meaning-making.[116] Both Piaget and Kegan are constructivist as they posit the continuous development of new structures from old ones and these new structures are progressively more complex, organized into increasingly adaptive higher order structures. I shall make this clear when I present Kegan's stage theory later. Kegan as a disciple of Piaget and Kegan's theory in the footsteps of Piaget would resonate with any of the above labels, though Kegan, as we shall see, rightly claims originality in the theory he has constructed.

Though it is just one among a myriad ego-development theories, Kegan's theory of the Evolving Self has depth and possibilities that hold out a promise for the future to provide an underlying ontology for understanding the human person and the dynamics of the process of growth and development throughout one's life span.

2.1. Kegan, the neo-Piagetian

Kegan does not call himself a Piagetian. Instead, he prefers to refer to himself as a neo-Piagetian. Kegan sees in Piaget not a psychologist per se and he does not regard Piaget's theory as a psychological theory *pur et simple*. Kegan finds in Piaget a new biology and a new epistemology in which to ground a new psychology of the person. Kegan draws our attention to the fact that Piaget maintained from the beginning of his career that he was not a psychologist but a "genetic epistemologist."[117] Piaget's life's work was centered more on the study of human knowledge acquisition than on the psychological development of the human person. Kegan, likewise, believes that his theory is not merely a psychological theory. He maintains that his theory, in fact, provides us not with developmental stages of one particular area of the person, such as cognition, affect, social, or moral, but of the whole person. His theory deals with the prior context of meaning-making that is at the root of the development of the whole person. Though Kegan takes his roots from Piaget, he does not find himself limited to the line of work that Piaget was committed to throughout his life. Instead, he ventures to push Piaget to an extent that Kegan's work seems to have transformed the Piagetian enterprise.

Heinz Werner,[118] a contemporary of Piaget, had also expounded a developmental theory similar to that of Piaget. However, he explained psychological development in terms of the "orthogenetic principle" of increasing differentiation and integration.[119] He held that an organism developed by means of slowly becoming different from the parent organism and then integrating these differences into the emerging organism. He maintained that an organism undergoes transformation as it outgrows a system of organization, which in turn becomes a subsystem or an element of the newly emerging system. While Werner spoke of differentiation and integration, Piaget expounded it in terms of decentration and equilibration. By this, Piaget meant that all organisms have an inner balance or equilibrium and as a result of interaction with the environment, this equilibrium is upset. However, the organism begins to find a new center and regains an equilibrium at a higher level. Piaget also explained each state that evolved as "a stage" in cognitive-development; as this has been acknowledged not only in cognitive-development, but in psycho-social development, Piaget himself is regarded as the father of this constructive-developmental paradigm. Kegan notes that the reason why these states are regarded as stages "is not just that they arrive in a regular sequence but that each, including the prior organization as the basic element *to be organized* in a new system, consists in a new equilibrial state balancing *subject* (the principle of organizing) with *object* (that which gets organized). Each stage of development, then, more than an era or period in the life-span, is a living subject-object relation, the cognate or root of a qualitatively different system of *knowing*."[120] When we make distinction between Werner and Piaget in regard to the way they explained psychological development, we know that Kegan most certainly is a protege of Piaget and not Werner.

2.2. Piaget – Kohlberg – Kegan

Piaget sees human intelligence as being rooted in a biological model. In this framework, there is no room for Cartesian dualism or the split between mind and body. There is a unity and coherence in the human person that calls for a single context from which biological, cognitive, affective, moral, and religious development have their origin. It was this unity of the human person that prompted Lawrence Kohlberg to study the moral development as a continuation of Piaget's developmental studies. Kegan accepts Piaget's and Kohlberg's view that there is an integral unity between the biological, cognitive, affective, moral and religious development of the human person.

In Kegan, we clearly detect what he emulates in Piaget: a passion for philosophy and biology. In Kegan's psychology, we see what he himself terms "a natural child of this distinguished marriage (between philosophy and biology)." [121] In Piaget, Kegan recognizes a genius who achieved more than he realized. Piaget is credited with ushering in a new era in cognitive-developmental psychology. His influence is seen in theories of moral and religious development in the works of Lawrence Kohlberg, James Fowler and others. Kegan notes that Piaget, Kohlberg and others "have taken the abstract notion of personal construction and made it almost palpable in revealing the apparently cross-culturally universal shape and sequence of 'logical, reliably interpretable, and systematically predictive theories'."[122]   Kegan sees in Piaget, an underlying epistemology in which to ground a new psychology of the human person. And that is precisely what Kegan does in his theory of the human person as the meaning-maker.

3. OTHER PSYCHOLOGICAL INFLUENCES

In Kegan's opinion, there are two psychological traditions that have had the greatest impact on theorists who see the person as meaning-maker. One is the Neo-Psychoanalytical tradition and the other the Existentialist-Phenomenological tradition.   He further distinguishes two sub-groups in the former: a) Neo-Psychoanalytic Ego Psychologies, represented by Anna Freud, Hartmann, Erikson and Kris and b) Neo-Psychoanalytic Object Relations Theories, exemplified in Fairbairn, Jacobsen, Winnicott, Mahler and Guntrip.   In the existential-phenomenological tradition, Kegan places Lecky, Maslow, May, Binswanger, Angyal, and Carl Rogers. Kegan notes that while acknowledging the crucial contribution each of these traditions have provided, we cannot be oblivious of the fact that each of them is in difficulty.[123] What Kegan proposes is not integration of these two traditions, but a third psychological tradition, the constructive-developmental approach, which does honor to the deepest convictions of both the existential and the dynamic personality psychologies.

Though the Neo-Psychoanalytic Ego psychologies and Neo-Psychoanalytic Object relations psychologies have their roots in Freud, they do not subscribe to the Freudian view of personality development as an internal process of maturation. Instead, they assert that personality development can take place only in the context of interaction between the organism and the environment. Kegan's neo-Piagetian approach shares this assertion and studies personality precisely in the process and stages of development of the person in the context of the interaction between the subject (organism) and the object (environment).

The Phenomenological-Existentialist perspective, as Kegan sees represented in Carl Rogers, was shaped by "the metaphors of twentieth-century evolutionary biology."[124] The first wave of psychology was prone to regard the human person as a mechanism that worked in accordance with definite laws of biology. While B.F. Skinner viewed the human person as being totally determined to respond to the supplied stimulus and nothing more, Rogers was averse to the mechanistic and deterministic conception of the development of the human person promoted by psychoanalysis and behaviorism. In using the biological metaphors, Rogers spoke of development as an intrinsic process of adaptation and growth. Like Abraham Maslow, Rogers regarded self-actualizing tendency as the prime motive in personality development. Kegan opines that this self-actualizing tendency presumes a basic unity to personality, "a unity best understood as a process rather than an entity."[125] Kegan's theory resonates with this conception of human development.

4. KEGAN'S ORIGINALITY

Having made Kegan's Piagetian roots clear, I must also warn readers that what eventually ensues as Kegan's theory is far from a mere elaboration or an expansion of what Piaget set out to do or what he actually proposed. Piaget had devoted his life to studying the cognitive development of children. He showed how children progress from the sensorimotor to the pre-operational to the concrete operational to the formal operational stages. After acknowledging his roots and his indebtedness to Piaget, Kegan asks, "Is there a stage of development beyond Piaget's formal operations?"[126] Kegan's answer to that question is that formal operations are not the end state in the process of psychological evolution. They should, in fact, be regarded as "an evolutionary state, the outcome of a long-lived ontogenetic process that has a specifiable and ongoing logic."[127] Kegan takes Piaget's theory farther even than what the father of constructive-development had probably envisioned. This will become obvious as one gains a grasp of Kegan's theory. Kegan himself writes, "Like Erikson, I have so changed the face of the theory in which I was steeped that although every one of the changes can be shown to grow out of, rather than depart from the theory's basic premises, one is still left with the slightly uncomfortable feeling that the father of the creation might not recognize the child as his own."[128]

4.1. Kegan's Metapsychology

However, as I have stated, Kegan finds that though the contributions of the Ego-Development psychologies, the Object-Relations psychologies and the Phenomenological-Existential psychologies are crucial to understanding the development of the human person, they fall short of an adequate and consistent theory of personality development. Kegan points out that each of these psychologies is distanced from the other intellectually and professionally. "The fact remains that no whole theory of personal functioning will be possible in the absence of some higher order psychology in which to integrate the wisdom of each."[129] There is a need for a metapsychology or a higher order psychology that will provide the framework for an adequate and consistent theory of personality development. Kegan's theory of meaning-making is his attempt to work out this metapsychology. Kegan's theory is keenly attentive to the origin, development, and process. He also formulates a personality theory that is sadly lacking in Roger's Existential-Phenomenological psychology.

This metapsychology purports to address several tensions within personality theories: the tensions between the psychological and social (those that Erikson, Jane Lovinger and several others address), between the past and present, between emotion and thought (as often psychoanalytic theory is regarded as theory about affect and Cognitive-developmental theory is regarded as a theory about cognition). As Kegan himself puts it, "My conception neither subsumes affectivity to the cognitive realm, as traditional Piagetians tend to do, nor makes intellectual life the offspring servant of affect, as psychoanalysis tends to do."[130]

This metapsychology draws from biological metaphors of growth, development and evolution; it is certainly focused on the person and stages of the person's growth and hence it is psychological; it is theoretical as it lays out the principles of embeddedness and letting-go as the foundation for personality development; it is empirical as it allows for observing and studying the development of persons using clearly distinguishable stages of growth. Above all, the biological model, the psycho-social development, and the personality theory, all flow from the philosophical basis that 'to be human is to be a meaning-maker,' and that 'being human essentially involves searching for the meaning that one is.' Kegan's framework addresses the forms and processes of meaning organization over the life span. The central phenomenon he studies is the evolution of the subject-object relations as "deep structures" by which the self organizes its interpersonal and intrapersonal experiencing. This entails attending to the formal or epistemological experience of subject-object evolution, the psychosocial concepts of "holding environments" which support or fail to support subject-object evolution, and the influence of intimate social relationships on the psychological disposition of the subject toward its objects.[131]

As we consider Kegan's stage theory of ego development, it is important to keep in mind what I have highlighted earlier: for Kegan, the master motion in personality is a lifelong process of evolution or adaptation, which according to Kegan is "an active process of increasingly organizing the relationship of the self to the environment."[132] This process of evolution is brought about by an innate propensity to make meaning of oneself in the context of one's environment. Kegan is convinced that this lifelong meaning-making of the evolving self is the common basis for explaining several developmental stage theories: Lawrence

Kohlberg's stages of moral reasoning, Robert Selman's stages of role-taking, and James Fowler's stages of faith.

5. CONSTRUCTIVE DEVELOPMENTALISM

Kegan brings together what he calls the "two Big Ideas" which according to him have influenced every aspect of intellectual life in the last hundred years: "constructivism (that persons or systems constitute or construct reality) and developmentalism (that organic systems evolve through eras according to regular principles of stability and change)."[133] Kegan calls his theory " constructive developmentalism," by which he means that his theory attends to the development of the activity of meaning-construction. He points out that both these ideas in some way hold that behind the form (or thing) there exists a process which creates it, or which leads to its coming into being."[134] For him, the human person is not just a being, i.e., something static, but a dynamic activity, the activity of meaning-making. To put it another way, the human person is not a mere *entity*, but rather a *process*.

5.1. Person as a Process and an Entity

Kegan points out that in any language, a noun is a naming word. It stands for a thing. It denotes an entity. A verb, on the other hand, is an action word. It denotes a process of activity. In the oriental way of thinking, a word that is a noun can also denote action or process of action. In Hebrew, for example, "davar," which means "word" denotes both the spoken word as well as what that spoken word brings about. In the first creation narrative in the book of Genesis, God utters the "word" and whatever that word signifies comes to existence. In English, and for that matter, in most modern occidental languages, "person," "self," and "ego" are all nouns and the western mind is brought up to think of the self or the person strictly as an entity. In Kegan's theory, we need to reframe what we mean by the person or the self. For Kegan, the person is as much a noun as a verb; an entity as well as a process.[135] The person is the system that makes meaning as well as the process of making-meaning. The one cannot be separated from the other. The two are inextricably linked. For Kegan, there is no other way of looking at the person or the self.[136]

5.2. Dialectical Context rather than Dichotomous Choice

When Robert Kegan developed his theory of ego development, he was fully aware that the field of ego or personality development was "somewhat encumbered by a number of poorly constructed metaphysical questions: which is to be taken as the master in personality, affect or cognition? or which should be the central focus, the individual or the social? or which should be the primary theater of investigation, the intrapsychic or the interpersonal? or even which is to be taken as the more powerful developmental framework, the psychoanalytic or the cognitive-structural?"[137] He was convinced that these questions present a *dichotomous choice* between two poles on a spectrum, which is neither beneficial nor valid.

An image that Kegan himself uses in another situation[138] might help us better understand his proposal to reconstruct the above questions from being posed primarily in a dichotomous choice to being engaged in a *dialectical context* in personality, which is philosophically prior to, and constructive of, these polarities. Let us consider a marble inside a glass cylinder that is lying on its side. If we roll the cylinder, we might ask ourselves at which end will the marble escape. We may focus our attention so exclusively on at which end the marble will come out, that we may end up regarding the cylinder as actually two openings connected by a glass tube. We may become oblivious of the fact that it is the tube that ultimately provides the possibility for the openings and not the other way about. If not for the cylinder there would be no openings. Similarly, there is a context of the human person, which is philosophically prior to, and constitutive of, the poles in the dichotomous choices presented above. For Kegan, this context is the evolution of meaning-making.

Central and quintessential to being human is to be engaged in a process of growth and development that is effected by the individual constantly constructing meaning of one's self through interaction with the environment. This evolution of meaning-making, according to Kegan, is philosophically antecedent to the diverse poles which are part and parcel of the human experience, such as cognition and affectivity, subjectivity and objectivity, intra-psychic and interpersonal, etc. Hence, in order to have a proper understanding of the human person, we must begin from this prior context before we speak of the dichotomous poles of human experience.

5.3. Embeddedness and Disembeddeness

A key to understanding Kegan's theory is the notion that he takes over from W.D.Winnicott. Winnicott had shown that human development in infants can come about only if there is what he called 'the holding environment.' By 'the holding environment' he meant a positive, affirming condition that must necessarily exist for any kind of human development to take place. Kegan insists that this holding environment is intrinsic, not only to infancy, but to the entire life cycle. "There is not one holding environment early in life, but a succession of holding environments, a life history of cultures of embeddedness."[139] Each stage in Kegan's theory is a different holding environment and plays a role in the development of the person. "Evolutionarily there is a sense in which the infant (and the person throughout life) climbs out of a psychological amniotic environment. Some part of that world in which the infant is embedded nourishes his gestation and assists in delivering him to a new evolutionary balance. I call that part the embeddedness culture, that most intimate of contexts out of which we repeatedly are recreated. I suggest that it serves at least three functions: It must hold on. It must let go. And it must stick around so that it can be reintegrated."[140] This embeddedness culture and its workings become quite evident in Kegan's stage theory.

We cannot talk about the holding environment or embeddedness without talking about disembeddedness. The person has to be slowly disembedded from one holding environment in order to be embedded in another. This is an integral part of the process of one's evolution. The embeddedness and the disembeddedness are in fact the human experience of tension between the longing for autonomy or individuality and the yearning for intimacy or inclusion. In each stage in Kegan's theory there is a movement from integration to separateness and separateness to integration. Kegan refers to what David Bakan termed the "duality of human experience" -- the yearnings for "communion" and "agency."[141] However, this whole evolutionary movement which involves embeddedness as well as disembeddedness is a very positive one. It signifies growth. "Growth itself is not alone a matter of separation and repudiation, of killing of the past. This is more a matter of transition. Growth involves as well the reconciliation, the recovery, the recognition of that which before was confused with the self."[142]

6. KEGAN'S FIRST PUBLISHED WORK IN CONTEXT

We need to point out that Kegan had published an earlier work, entitled *The Sweeter Welcome*.[143] There is a strong possibility that readers overlook or even disregard the connection between Kegan's first book published in 1976 and his other two works merely because *The Sweeter Welcome* was written before Kegan formulated his theory. It is my contention that what Kegan deals with in his first book has an intrinsic connection with his theory and, in fact, is very crucial to a comprehensive understanding of Kegan's theory. As a psychologist, Kegan is fully aware that he must limit the extent of his study to the empirical world. The claims of his theory are justifiably restricted to observable evolution of the self. Both *The Evolving Self* and *In Over Our Heads* demonstrate Kegan's acute insights as a psychologist and he does not venture beyond the confines of psychology. It is significant to note that Kegan did not write *The Sweeter Welcome* as a psychologist. He was neither attempting to establish a psychological theory nor validate one as he did in his other two books. *The Sweeter Welcome* is written from the perspective of a literary critic, a student of Martin Buber's existentialism and an explorer of Hasidic mysticism. Here we have the opportunity to enter the world of Kegan, the literary critic, the philosopher and the theologian. For the purposes of this work, I am particularly interested in eliciting the link between his psychological theory and his overall view of the human person in the context of the transcendent. A close look at *The Sweeter Welcome* will provide us with that critical link. However, as the focus of this chapter is the person as the meaning-maker, we shall leave the discussion on *The Sweeter Welcome* to the next chapter and essentially narrow our inquiry here to Kegan's *The Evolving Self,* In *Over Our Heads,* and a few relevant articles that he has written.

7. KEGAN'S STAGE THEORY OF PERSONALITY DEVELOPMENT

Kegan's thesis can be simply stated thus: to be human is to be a meaning-maker. He presents this thesis in *The Evolving Self.* He maps out the evolution of the self in five clearly describable stages. Kegan and his colleagues developed an instrument, "Subject-Object Interview," in the years following the publication of *The Evolving Self.* This instrument was administered to several hundred participants. A companion research manual was developed to accompany the instrument and to test the validity of the theory. After some twelve years of research, observation, and study, Kegan published *In Over Our Heads*, in which he staunchly stands by the theory he had presented in his earlier work.[144]

Basic to Kegan's theory is that throughout life every individual progresses through a series of subject-object relations which aids the individual to construct personal meaning. Kegan insists that these subject-object relations are not mere abstractions as they "take form in actual human relations and social contexts."[145] It is also important to understand that the subject-object relation is not something that is permanent or static. It is dynamic and evolutionary. At each stage of Kegan's theory it is evident that "these subject-object distinctions are in fact tenuous, frail, precarious states. They are balances, ...they can tip over. They are truces, ...chaos and a state of siege hang around the corner."[146] As we move from one stage to the next, we change not only the relations between the subject and object, we radically change the very subject and the object. It is in the realization of the changed subject that the self evolves.

What defines the logic of the person's meanings (psychologic) is arrived at by clarifying what is 'self' and what is the 'other.' In Kegan's understanding, "what is self and what is other may be a question of the person's 'biology,' but it is equally a question of the person's 'philosophy': what is the subject-object relationship the person has become in the world?"[147] Now, we can turn our attention to each stage in Kegan's evolution of the meaning-making self.

7.1. Stage zero: Incorporative Stage

Infants react to light, warmth, touch, hunger, etc. They are capable of moving their arms and legs. They respond through their senses and motion. However, they have no differentiation of object and subject. In fact, they have no sense of anything outside of themselves. Kegan's view is "birth itself as the beginning of the transition out of the first evolutionary position. What must be most dramatic about this new world for the infant is an end to this harmony."[148] Symbiotic relationship with the primary care-giver illustrates the infant's lack of subject-object differentiation. The child's survival instinct is tied up with its physiological needs (Maslow); looking at it from Piaget's cognitive development, the incorporative self is at the sensorimotor stage. As Kegan finds no object to relate to, he designates this as stage 0. Kegan denotes the transformation from stage 0 to stage 1 as the birth of the object. According to him, it is an attempt to bring about qualitatively new object relations.

7.2. Stage one: Impulsive Stage

The infant was a bundle of reflexes. As he grows, instead of being those reflexes, he has these reflexes. There is an evolution of the self that is different from the reflexes. The reflexes have become an object to the self. At this stage, the child identifies the object with his perception of the object. Kegan suggests that this corresponds to Freud's preoedipal years (ages 3-5) and the structure of Piaget's pre-operational stage. The child, at this stage, is embedded in his perceptions and impulses. The self, here, is one with the impulses. In this stage, two separate impulses cannot be coordinated or held together. This would explain why the toddler is unable to experience ambivalence. "The impulses *are* the self, are themselves the context."[149] This would explain why a toddler has little impulse control and the proverbial "terrible twos" makes sense in Kegan's theory of meaning-making. A new self has evolved which has not lost its old self of reflexes, but has made it the objective-pole of his meaning-making self. A new evolutionary truce has come about.

Kegan denotes the transformation from stage 1 to stage 2 as the birth of the role. Psychodynamically, it is a period when a child, who had thus far identified him/herself with his/her impulses and perceptions, begins to bring those impulses and perceptions under her own regulation. The child has evolved into a new self, a new subjectivity.[150] The child is moving from a fantasy orientation to a reality orientation. "In bringing his impulses and perceptions under his own regulation, the child creates a self that he sees as distinct and in business for itself; in its fullest flush of confidence this is the bike-riding, money-managing, card-trading, wristwatch-wearing, pack-running, code-cracking, self-waking, puzzle-solving nine- or ten-year-old known to all of us."[151] In the transition from stage 1 to 2, which normally would transpire between the ages of five and seven, there is a shift in the psychological and social world of the child. "The younger child's life is filled with fantasy and fantasy about the fantastic (e.g., being Superman); the older child takes an interest in things as they are, and fantasy life is about things that actually could be (e.g., being a doctor). The younger child makes a decision of right and wrong on the basis of what an outside authority deems to be right and wrong, and orients his thinking to the consequence of an act; the older child makes decisions of right and wrong on the basis of what benefits himself and orients to the intentions that underlie the consequences."[152] There is a close correspondence in transition from punishment and obedience orientation stage to Instrumental orientation stage in Kohlberg's theory of moral-reasoning.

7.3. Stage two: Imperial Stage

As the child grows, s/he realizes that his/her perceptions and impulses are not identical with her 'self.' This gives rise to having a separate world of her own. She is capable of distinguishing between her own goals and the intent of others. "The child can step out of the concrete bounds of the self, thus creating 'two-way' reciprocity."[153]   Kegan says that the child's new subject-object relationship can be seen in the terms of the construction of the role. The new role is a capacity to take the role of another person, both cognitively and socially. In fact, this new subject-object relationship, characterized in terms of the role of the 'child' in relation to that of a 'parent' can be seen in the context of the self, not as a bundle of impulses, but as something that the self is distinct from. The self is no more those impulses, but has those impulses. It is at this stage that we can see the emergence of a self concept. The earlier sense of self, *that* I am, has evolved to a sense of self, *what* I am. At this stage, there is yet to evolve the sense of self, *who* I am.

There is a certain sense of control over one's impulses. It gives the child the ability to have a certain amount of power over his/her impulses. S/he is the agent of his/her impulses. He experiences a sense of autonomy. Kegan points out that "[t]he end of Kohlberg's first moral stage, where authority is all-powerful and right by virtue of its *being* authority, is probably brought on by this construction of one's own authority."[154]

If the self is disembedded from the impulses, what is the new context for the self? The self has become identified with his/her own needs. In other words, one's interests and wishes are the subjective pole of the meaning-making self. What the self wants is what the self is.

7.4. Stage three: Interpersonal Stage

The self becomes disembedded from the needs, wants, and interests with which he had identified himself. He no longer is his needs, wishes, and interests. He has these needs, wishes, and interests. They have become the objective pole of the meaning-making self. A new subjective pole has emerged. The self has begun to move out of its own self. There is an ability to "coordinate, or integrate, one need system with another, and in so doing, I bring into being that need-mediating reality which we refer to when we speak of mutuality."[155] Adolescence is the transitional state where this evolutionary stage begins to emerge. The adolescent struggles to engage in a conversation with peers and adults to be embedded in mutuality. It is not an easy task to perform, especially for an adolescent who is still establishing his self-concept. The adolescent's self-image is bound to how the other people view him or like him. It must be noted that this stage is not exclusively an adolescent's world. Some adults find themselves entrenched in this stage. They still find their identity as being dependent on how others see them, view them, or perceive them. As Kegan states, "This balance is 'interpersonal' but it is not 'intimate,' because what might appear to be intimacy here is the self's *source* rather than its aim. There is no self to share with another; instead the other is required to bring the self into being. Fusion is not intimacy. If one can feel manipulated by the imperial balance, one can feel devoured by the interpersonal one."[156]

7.5. Stage four: Institutional Stage

The self has been in search of identity. During adolescence identity is found in belonging to a group. Relationship with other teens is of prime importance. In fact, there is a sense of identifying oneself with one's relationships. As the self seeks her own identity, she slowly becomes aware that she is not her relationships; rather she has relationships. In Kegan's own words,

> In separating itself from the context of interpersonalism, meaning-evolution authors a self, which maintains a coherence across a shared psychological space and so achieves an identity. This authority -- sense of self, self-dependence, self-ownership -- is its hallmark. In moving from 'I am my relationships' to 'I have relationships,' there is now somebody who is doing this having, the new I, who, in coordinating or reflecting upon mutuality, brings into being a kind of psychic institution (*in+statuere*: to set up; *statutum*: law, regulation; as in 'statute' and 'state').[157]

In stage 3, the self experienced emotions either from one's own perspective or that of the other. That sense of ambivalence gives way to a mutuality which integrates to some extent, making it possible to hold both the perspectives simultaneously. In stage 4, the self becomes regulative of its feelings and this is the crucial difference between the interpersonal and the institutional stages.

Having moved the shared context over from subject to object, the feelings which arise out of interpersonalism do not reflect the structure of my equilibrative knowing and being, but are, in fact, reflected upon by that structure. The context for the institutional stage is the construction of norms, roles, self-concept, and auto-regulation, which maintain the psychic institution. This makes it possible for the self to evolve its legal, societal, normative system.

We must insist, once again, that the institutional self, instead of losing its interpersonal relationships of stage 3, in fact, appropriates them "to the new context of their place in the maintenance of a personal system."[158] Kegan sees here a parallel with Erikson's basis for identity formation, because Kegan's stage 4 is ideological; it establishes a system, a truth for a group or class. Mutuality which was the directive force in stage 3 has given way once again to the mediacy of controlling or regulating the interpersonal.

7.6. Stage five: Interindividual Stage

In the Institutional balance, the self becomes capable of owning himself rather than being under the control of the various parts of himself. Kegan points out that this very strength is also a limitation on the self, because in stage 4, the self is not the organizer but "an administrator in the narrow sense of the word, a person whose meanings are derived out of the organization, rather than deriving the organization out of her meaning/principle/purpose/reality. Stage 4 has no 'self', no 'truth', before which it can bring the operational constraints of the organization, because its 'self,' its 'source,' its 'truth,' is invested within these operational constraints."[159]

In bringing about self-government in stage 4, there is a possibility that the ego may regard the psychic institution as an end itself. The evolution that occurs in stage 5, is that the ego which formerly was the organization, is becoming the organizer who directs the psychic institution. The self is the mover, rather than the moved. The self recognizes other selves as independent egos with whom she can interrelate as individuals. There is a sense of oneself and others as "value-originating, system-generating, history-making individuals."[160] The question that arises is: has the sense of connectedness that emerged in earlier stages given way to a separateness, a distance, from other people? Though it is true that the self in stage 5 has an individuality that surpasses the sense of self and a greater realization of distinctness from others in earlier stages, the connectedness with others has also progressed. In stage 2, the ego was capable of relating to others as fellow-instrumentalists; in stage 3, there was a potential for fusion with others as partners; in stage 4, there was a connectedness with others as loyalists. However, in stage 5, the mutuality with others is one of respecting each one's individuality and forming a community of individuals who are self-directing. In stage 3, the self was derived from others and hence was called "interpersonal." In stage 5, the self is brought to others and hence is called "interindividual." In stage 3, the coming together was a fusion of individuals; in stage 5, it is a commingling that guarantees distinct identities. There was hardly a possibility for intimacy; and this possibility is a reality in stage 5 because there is a self to share. There is a possibility for communion because there is an individuality that is differentiated enough to bring about an interindividuality.

8. CONCLUSION

Kegan's stages are consistent with his theory. At each of the stages, Kegan reiterates that the master motion in personality is a lifelong process of evolution or adaptation. Throughout his exposition of the theory, Kegan keeps returning to this master motion in personality. He maintains that this is the underlying epigenesis of growth and development. At each stage, the self is engaged in "an active process of increasingly organizing the relationship of the self to the environment. The relationship gets better organized by increasing differentiation of the self from the environment and thus by increasing integrations *of* the environment."[161] As a result of this adaptation, the self has to relinquish a familiar sense of equilibrium and struggle to adjust to a new balance. Kegan points out that "every new balance represents a capacity to listen to what before one could only hear irritably, and the capacity to hear irritably what before one could hear not at all."[162] Crucial to understanding Kegan's theory is that the self does not lose its previous grasp of self, it enhances the way or the manner in which it grasps the self. Kegan's words are powerful, "The hallmark of every rebalancing is that the past, which may during transition be repudiated, is not finally rejected, but reappropriated."[163]

Kegan himself sums up his theory thus:

> Every equilibrium amounts to a kind of 'theory' of the prior stage; this is another way of speaking about subject moving to the object, or structure becoming content. Stage 2 is a theory of impulse; the impulses are organized or ordered by the needs, wishes, or interests. Stage 3 is a 'theory' of needs; they are ordered by that which is taken as prior to the interpersonal relationships. Stage 4 is a kind of theory of interpersonal relationships; they are rooted in and reckoned by institutions. Stage 5 is a theory of the institutional; the institutional is ordered by the new self which is taken as superior to the institutional.[164]

In his *In Over our Heads*, Kegan extended his investigation beyond the study of the individual to an examination of contemporary culture. He explains that his purpose in this work is "to look at the curriculum of modern life in relation to the capacities of the adult mind."[165] Kegan's interest has always been meaning-making and the evolution of consciousness. While in *The Evolving Self*, Kegan's focus was on the psychological phenomenon of the evolution of the self, in *In Over our Heads*, his attention turns to what he calls the cultural phenomenon--"the mental demands implicit in the so-called postmodern prescriptions for adult living."[166] In investigating this cultural phenomenon, Kegan considers not only people's agendas, but also their changing capacities. Kegan's many years of research, whether it is in the arena of the psychological or the cultural phenomenon, have convinced him of the validity of his original theory. In fact, he is unequivocal in stating that, "the theory's central premises and distinctions remain unchanged, but they are clearer and better supported."[167] In *In Over our Heads*, Kegan, while using the stage theory as an analytical tool, expounds four categories of consciousness. These categories of consciousness are important to understand how individuals and societies progressively move from one level of consciousness to the next level in response to the demands made on the individual or society. Though Kegan's exposition of the four categories of consciousness adds another dimension to his theory, it does not alter his basic theory. It would not benefit us to go into the details of his categories of consciousness in this work.

Kegan's theory has a distinct advantage over many other theories of personality development because his theory is holistic. Kegan writes, "My conception neither subsumes affectivity to the cognitive realm, as traditional Piagetians tend to do, nor makes intellectual life the offspring servant of affect, as psychoanalysis tends to do."[168] Each stage of development addresses the whole person and not a particular function of a person. Kegan is fully aware of his original contribution. He writes, "Building on the work of Piaget and those who came after him, I took the idea of such principles of mental organization and extended its 'breath' (beyond thinking to affective, interpersonal, and intrapersonal realms) and its 'length' (beyond childhood and adolescence to adulthood)."[169]

In light of the works of Carol Gilligan and Jean Baker Miller, many women raised a number of issues regarding the validity of Kegan's theory for women's development. Already in *The Evolving Self* Kegan refers to Gilligan's *In a Different Voice*[170] and points out that theories of personality tended to emphasize differentiation as what signifies growth and development while underplaying integration which focuses attention on dependency and mutuality. Kegan was convinced that as his model is in pursuit of the psychological meaning and experience of evolution, which is "intrinsically about differentiation *and* integration,"[171] it is less prone to favor growth and development of the male over the female. However, ten years later, Kegan admits that there was a lack of clarity in addressing the issue of women's development in his earlier work.[172] In essence the question can be posed thus: Is not a theory of consciousness essentially validating a typically male orientation and presenting it as the norm for development across the board for men and women? In response to this criticism,

Kegan points out that consciousness in men and women is not to be construed as an epistemological difference. It is only a stylistic difference. Kegan compares it to the Myers-Briggs Type Indicator, which shows simply the preferences about the way we experience reality. Kegan argues that we must not confuse stylistic differences, which are neither better nor more valuable, with content, which brings with it a hierarchical ordering as in the case of cognition over affect. This is an important difference and Kegan is right in maintaining that his theory is non-preferential and is equally applicable to men and women.

Kegan chooses a potent, graphic representation of his theory of ego development. Consonant with the exposition of his theory, Kegan declares that a linear representation of development falls short of the dynamism and progressive integration of previous stages. A spiral or a helix is a more vibrant representation. A helix indicates that "we move back and forth in our struggle with this lifelong tension; that our balances are slightly *im*balanced….The model makes graphically clear the way we revisit old issues but at a whole new level of complexity."[173] The helix or the spiral model adds vitality and energy to Kegan's theory.

Kegan's theory is psychological. In his two major works he writes as a psychologist and does not entertain the realm of the spiritual or the religious. We will explore the spiritual and religious possibilities for his theory in the next chapter. However, I would like to draw attention to some salient comments in *The Evolving Self* that will be an appropriate way of leading us into the next chapter. Kegan presents the human experience of embeddedness and disembeddedness as crucial to his theory. As I pointed out earlier, Kegan concurs with David Bakan when he speaks of the yearning for 'communion' and 'agency' to describe what he calls 'the duality of human experience.' Kegan maintains that old-fashioned words like yearn, plea, long for, mourn, etc. convey this longing for communion and agency. In Kegan's words,

> Those who are religiously oriented will note that the same old-fashioned language finds its way into prayer, and that much liturgy and scripture is an expression of one or the other of these two longings. I think of

Schleiermacher's 'ultimate dependence' on the one hand and Luther's 'Here I Stand' on the other; of the fervent communalism of Hasidism on the one hand and the lonely Job, talking to (ever cursing) the Lord, on the other.[174]

.

CHAPTER IV
SELF-TRANSCENDING MEANING-MAKER

1. INTRODUCTION

1.1. Source and Goal of Self-Transcendence

In this chapter, we shall focus our attention not merely on the subject as self-transcendent or the person as the meaning-maker, but on the self-transcending meaning-maker. Our purpose is to see the integral link between Lonergan's notion of the subject as self-transcendent and Kegan's person as the meaning-maker. The two complement each other and lend us a framework for doing Christian anthropology. It is through the process of meaning-making that a person transcends one's present grasp of the self and evolves continuously to unravel the mystery that s/he is. In this chapter, we ask who or what is the source of this self-transcendence? And who or what is the goal that draws the self-transcending subject?

1.2. Pushing beyond the empirical

In the second chapter, we showed that Lonergan's self-transcendent subject is the existential subject. This existential subject, through intentional and conscious operations, ever more fully self-actualizes through what Lonergan terms the "the unfolding of a single thrust, the eros of the human spirit."[175] In that chapter, we began our discussion with the subject's world of immediacy, "the world of what is felt, touched, grasped, sucked, seen, heard.... it is the world of immediate experience, of the given as given, of image, and affect without any perceptible intrusion from insight or concept, reflection, or judgment, deliberation, or choice."[176] We concluded the chapter with the subject's world mediated by meaning, a world that is progressively expanding and transcending one's world of immediate experience. Later in this chapter we will develop the notion of horizon and the radical shifts in horizon which Lonergan calls conversions. These conversions, for Lonergan, are authentic instances of self-transcendence.

In the chapter on Kegan we made no direct reference to self-transcendence. The question is, if self-transcendence is crucial to the thesis developed in this work, what relevance does our treatment of Kegan's theory have in our context. To put it in another way, if we cannot show the connection between Kegan's theory of human person as meaning-maker and self-transcendence, and consequently, how that connection would contribute to the study of Christian anthropology, the third chapter would have been a futile exercise. Our contention is that though in our discussion of Kegan's ego-development theory, there was no explicit reference to self-transcendence, there is an implicit acceptance of self-transcendence as the key to the constructive-developmental movement of the person as reflected in Kegan's theory.

Though neither Lonergan nor Kegan had initially set out to outline a philosophy of the human person, their entire body of work rests on their respective view of the human person. It must also be clear from the previous two chapters that I have chosen to present Kegan's view of the human person and Lonergan's human subject separately without attempting to link them or relate them in any manner whatsoever. This was explicitly intended as a means to ensure that their views were presented as they themselves had propounded them. For the purposes of this work, it is now necessary to demonstrate how their views of the human person provide us with a starting point for Christian anthropology. That is the purpose of this chapter.

1.3. Bringing Lonergan and Kegan Together

Is there a common thread that runs through Kegan's human person and Lonergan's human subject? I have presented Kegan's theory from the clinical psychologist's perspective, because he developed his theory in that discipline and he continues to work as a clinical psychologist. Lonergan was primarily a philosopher and a theologian. I have presented his view of the human subject from a philosophical and theological perspective. How can we use their singular contributions to their disciplines and show their relevance to the framework for Christian anthropology presented here?

Both Kegan and Lonergan in their respective works have demonstrated that they transcend the confines of their own disciplines. Though they are primarily engaged in their own field of expertise, both of them relied on other disciplines and drew heavily from various fields of knowledge to build up their own thinking. It is precisely their broad base of knowledge that makes it possible for them to provide an organon for their discipline. Lonergan took upon himself the task of attempting to provide a method, as he called it, for theology and, in fact, for all branches of knowledge. Lonergan has been credited by scholars[177] to have drawn attention to the works of Aristotle, Aquinas, and Newton as being the inspiration for him to bring about a new framework for knowledge. Kegan attempted to bring together the insights of Piaget, Erickson, Selman, Kohlberg, Maslow, and Loevinger under the common ground of the balances of self and the other. Although Kegan himself has never claimed to have worked out an organon for our times, he does illustrate convincingly that most of the important developmental theories: the cognitive development theory of Piaget, the perspective-taking development theory of Selman, the moral development theory of Kohlberg, the psycho-social development theory of Erickson, the ego development theories of Maslow and Loevinger can be seen from the unifying perspective of Kegan's own theory of the evolving self.[178] Arguably, we can say that Kegan has presented an organon for an understanding of the self for counselors, therapists, clients, and developmental theorists.

Another important common thread that runs through the works of Lonergan and Kegan is that both of them were greatly influenced by the work of Piaget. In the case of Lonergan it was an obvious influence, while in the case of Kegan it was an overwhelming guiding force. Lonergan openly acknowledged his indebtedness to Piaget in several of his works. It is most clearly stated in *Insight* and in *Method in Theology* and several of his writings in the three Collections. Kegan dubs himself a neo-Piagetian. He rooted his whole theory in the basic epistemology that Piaget had worked out. In the end Kegan had moved Piaget's theory to realms which Piaget himself did not consider including. There can be no doubt that the genius of Piaget plays a significant role in the work of both Lonergan and Kegan.

2. KEGAN'S REPLY TO THE EXISTENTIAL DILEMMA

2.1. Response of Alienation: Nietzsche and Sartre

It is my contention that though Kegan has outlined his theory in terms of psychology and expounded it in terms of the empirical, there is an underlying assumption regarding the human spirit that undergirds his view of the human person. Kegan's very first book may provide the clue to his understanding of the human person. *In The Sweeter Welcome*, Kegan was quite evidently gripped by the mysticism of Hasidism. The book was a tool to give expression to his firm conviction that the apparent sensible, tangible expressions of the human do not exhaust the totality of who the human person is. In a world that has been besieged by the nihilism of Nietzsche and Sartre, the transcendence of the human spirit has been exiled. Nietzsche and Sartre had raised the question: given that there is nothing up there, meaning divinity and the transcendent, what is down here, meaning humanity and the immanent? Sartre was convinced that humans were strangers to each other; humans were condemned to nothingness and meaninglessness and human existence is utter absurdity. Consequently the logical answer to the above question that Nietzsche and Sartre arrived at was nihilism and alienation. Kegan is convinced that there are alternate answers.

2.2. Response of Accommodation: Camus

Albert Camus accepted that there was nothing up there, but he offered a different reply to "so what is down here?" Human life may be absurd, but it is not meaningless or unsatisfying. Kegan calls this the accommodationist reply. Kegan cites how Camus reinterpreted the tale of Sisyphus. The classical tale of Sisyphus narrates how the gods had condemned Sisyphus to push a huge boulder up a steep slope of a hill, only to see it roll down the other side. His entire life was consumed by the futile task of rolling the boulder up the hill on the one side, seeing it roll down the other side, and pushing it up the hill once again. Camus' reinterpretation was that the life of Sisyphus may appear to be futile and sterile, but not totally meaningless, as the very struggle can be fulfilling to the human heart.[179] Kegan quotes Camus, "Sisyphus concludes that all is well. The universe, though without a master, seems neither sterile nor futile. Each atom of that stone, each mineral flake of that night-filled mountain, in itself forms a world. The struggle itself is enough to fill a man's heart."[180] Kegan is far from satisfied with the replies of alienation and accommodation, which he terms the answers of "spiritual circularity and spiritual dissipation."[181]

2.3. Response of Affirmation: Buber, Bellow, and Malamud

Kegan contends there is yet another answer to the existential question. This time, he points to the novels of Saul Bellow and Bernard Malamud, who according to Kegan, lend their literary voices to the philosophy of Martin Buber. Rejecting the answers of alienation and accommodation to the questions, "Given that there is nothing up there, what is down here?" Kegan writes, "There is another answer. There is affirmation: 'Everything! It's all down here. We may be living without the vertical. We may live on the horizontal. But the horizontal is the holy!'"[182] The here-and-now, the human, the immanent is no more to be seen as dichotomous with the beyond, the divine and the transcendent. The beyond is within us. This, in brief, is what Kegan highlights in the philosophy of Buber. It must be pointed out that this is also the answer of Abraham Heschel and Isaac Peretz. It is, in fact, the expression of the spirituality of neo-Hasidism. And that is what Kegan sets out to present in his very first published work as the alternate answer to the dichotomy of 'being-in-itself' and 'being-for-itself' that Sartre had presented.[183]

2.4. Response of Transcendence-in-immanence: Kegan

It is my contention that though Kegan's theory does not base itself in or link itself to the spirituality of new-Hasidism, this answer of affirmation, as Kegan calls it in *The Sweeter Welcome*, is implicit in his theory of the Evolving Self. If meaning-making is the underlying structure in the human person, and if Kegan insists that it is only through meaning-constructing that the human person evolves from the lower stages of development to the higher in a spiraling, forward-reaching, ever-progressive movement, what he is, in fact, expounding is a theory of the self in transcendence. At each stage, the self, through meaning-constructing, reaches out of itself and beyond its present consciousness of self and becomes that which it is tending towards or reaching out for.

Kegan, the clinical psychologist, is concerned with the empirical and his theory lays out the observable in each of the stages and the conclusion that can be derived from those observations. However, there is deeper issue at stake. What is the source of this transcendence? What is it that drives the human to move from the lower stages of self to the higher? These questions are for the philosopher and the theologian to grapple with. It is my conviction that in *The Sweeter Welcome*, Kegan, the philosopher and theologian, has, in retrospect, provided some clues to direct us in seeking an answer to the cause and source of the movement of self-transcendence in the progressively developing human person. The movement of self-transcendence is to be found in the immanence of the human experience. The divine is to be found within the human; the transcendent within the immanent.

3. *THE SWEETER WELCOME*

Though it is not my intention to offer an elaborate analysis of *The Sweeter Welcome*, I think it necessary to dwell briefly on some salient aspects of the book to substantiate my position regarding Kegan's underlying implication of the transcendence-in-immanence for his psychological theory of the Evolving Self.

At the very outset, it must be stated that Kegan's express intention in writing his first book was definitely not to lay out a philosophical or theological basis for his subsequent psychological theory. It was probably the farthest thing on his mind then. It may also be stated that even while Kegan was developing his theory of the evolving self, he was probably not thinking of transcendence-in-immanence as the grounding for his theory. He was researching and presenting his research purely as a clinical psychologist. It must also be made clear that Kegan himself has nowhere claimed that his psychological theory is based on the notion of transcendence-in-immanence. It is entirely a conclusion that I have arrived at from studying Kegan's theory and finding the link so very obvious. What I am doing is to explicate what I think is implicit in Kegan's earlier work and later theory.

In *The Sweeter Welcome*, Kegan sets out to study some of the novels of two Jewish novelists, Saul Bellow and Bernard Malamud. He presents them as transcending "their own materials to offer a new voice for contemporary fiction."[184] It is interesting that Kegan starts the book with a few disclaimers: he stresses that the book is not a study of Jewish novelists, nor even a study of Bellow or Malamud, nor a critical treatment of the form of the novels presented. Then, what is the book about? Kegan himself gives us the answer: "It is a study of those books (novels) in light of Buber's thought."[185] As I have explained earlier, Kegan was not principally interested in the novels, but the new voice of "affirmation" - affirmation of the transcendent within our midst. Kegan borrows E.M. Foster's idea that these novels " 'have gods,' 'a song,' a certain 'tone of voice,'...such novels are 'more than time or people or logic or any of their derivatives, more even than Fate."[186] In short, the main purpose of Kegan's work is to present, as already mentioned, a voice of affirmation of the transcendence-in-immanence as a viable alternative to the voices of alienation and accommodation that dominated the earlier part of the twentieth century as a response to the challenge of existentialism.

It should be evident that though Bellow and Malamud, each has his own tone of voice, it is not so much their voices that Kegan is interested in, but in their voices resounding in unison with the philosophy of Martin Buber. I shall refrain from going into each of the novels of Bellow and Malamud as Kegan himself does within *The Sweeter Welcome*. I shall, instead, turn to some of the insights of Buber and neo-Hasidism that I feel are intimately linked to Kegan's interest in the transcendence-in-immanence.

4. HASIDISM AND BUBER

Buber's philosophy cannot be understood apart from Hasidism. Hence, first, a word about Hasidism. Hasidism, derived from the Hebrew word, *"Hasid"* which means "a pious one," was a Jewish movement founded in the villages of Poland by Israel ben Eliezer in the middle of the eighteenth century. It was intended to help Jews live according to the thought and folkways of ancient Judaism. It sought to resist change and vigorously preserve the medieval customs and outlooks of their ancestors. Hasidism emphasized the joyful worship of God in the here and now, in this world and in this life. Buber, who, in his younger days, had been captivated by the vitality and dynamism of Nietzsche and then the philosophy of Kierkegaard, was irrevocably influenced by this eighteenth century movement and was responsible in large measure for bringing attention to it in the twentieth century. This is the reason why the thought of Buber is constantly referred to as neo-Hasidism.

It is crucial to point out how Kegan explains neo-Hasidism in the context of our previous discussion of a contemporary answer to the existential question of "If there is nothing up there? What is down here?" According to Kegan, "Neo-Hasidism, historically and temperamentally, represents the flowering of existentialism -- whose seeds were originally sown when Hebrew met Hellene."[187] Kegan, then cites Harvey Cox to demonstrate the drastic change brought about through this meeting. Cox's analysis in a nutshell is, "The impact of Hebrew faith on the Hellenistic world was to temporalize the dominant perception of reality. The world became history. *Cosmos* became *aeon*; *mundus* ('world' in a space sense) became *saeculum* ('world' in a time sense)."[188] Kegan goes on to elaborate on the dichotomy between Hebraism and Hellenism from the standpoint of Hasidism. He lists four pairs of dichotomies, which William Barrett had first enumerated in his essay "The Testimony of Modern Art"[189]:

1. The ideal man of Hebraism is the man of faith; the ideal man of Hellenism is the man of reason.

2. The Hebrew viewed man in his wholeness and not in his separate parts. They paid scant attention to the universal and the abstract and maintained the focus of vision to the concrete, particular individual. The Greeks, on the other hand, were the discoverers of the universal, the abstract and timeless essences, forms, and ideas.

3. While the Greek idealized detachment, the Hebrew extolled commitment, the passionate involvement with one's mortal being, which was both flesh and spirit at the same time, and with his offspring, tribe, and God.

4. Greeks placed the intellect on a pedestal, defining the human as the animal of connected logical disclosure. Hebrews, on the other hand, saw intellect and reason as the downfall of the human, the pride of fools. They acknowledged the poverty of the intellect, which could not understand the ultimate issues of life.

Kegan cites Barrett, "The features of Hebraic man are those which existential philosophy has attempted to exhume and bring to the reflective consciousness of our time."[190] Kegan adds, "And existentialism has done this, but it has done this inconclusively. The answers of alienation and accommodation emphasize to an extent, the Hebraic directions."[191] However, Kegan points out that it is the answer of Hasidism, the affirmative answer, itself a child of Hebraism, which can bring back the Hebrew ideal to the reflective consciousness of our times. The discovery of meaning and significance in the every day life is the crux of the affirmative answer of Hasidism and is a far cry from alienation and accommodation. Buber states that the fundamental principle of Hasidism can be expressed as follows: "God can be beheld in each thing and in each pure deed."[192] This is as simple as we can state the notion of transcendence-in-immanence.

5. *SWEETER WELCOME* AND *THE EVOLVING SELF*

Kegan's theory of the evolving self resonates with the view expressed by Buber in *Hasidism and the Modern Man*: "All that man possesses conceals sparks which belong to the root of his soul and wish to be elevated by him to their origin...in the era before creation these sparks had fallen into all things and are now imprisoned in them until ever again a man uses a thing in holiness and thus liberates the sparks that it conceals."[193] This is the crux of Hasidism: the hallowing of the everyday. Buber elaborates, "The issue is not to attain a new type of acting which, owing to its object, would be sacred or mystical; the issue is to do the one appointed task, the common obvious tasks of daily life according to their truth and according their meaning."[194] It is not surprising that Kegan quotes these words of Buber in his very first publication, providing us with a framework for understanding meaning construction as the basis for the evolving self.

6. LINKING KEGAN AND LONERGAN

Thus far in this chapter, we have been pushing Kegan's understanding of the human beyond his psychological theory. In chapter three, we had laid out his basic view of the human as being an integral whole. According to Kegan earlier theories of ego development were "somewhat encumbered by a number of poorly constructed metaphysical questions: which is to be taken as the master in personality, affect or cognition? Or which should be the central focus, the individual or the social? Or what should be the primary theater of investigation, the intrapsychic or the interpersonal? Or even which is to be taken as the more powerful developmental framework, the psychoanalytic or the cognitive-structural?"[195] Kegan's view of the human person presupposes the context of meaning-making as being philosophically prior to, and constitutive, of the poles in the dichotomous choices. In this chapter, we have used Kegan's earlier work, *The Sweeter Welcome*, to make a logical inference that this prior context which is constitutive of the self and which makes possible the self's transcendence is in fact the drive to reach the God who is in heart of each human being.

Our next task is to show how this unifying move to self-transcendence as the drive to reach the God within our hearts is in fact how Lonergan presents his understanding of the human person. In chapter two, we looked at Lonergan's philosophical underpinnings for his view of what it means to be human. In this chapter, we will show that the exigence to transcendence is realized through a ever-progressive movement that involves intellectual, affective, moral, and religious conversions. The culmination of human transcendence is religious conversion which Lonergan terms an other-worldly falling-in-love. Ultimately, the human is destined to be in love with the Transcendent. This is the reason why the human person is constantly seeking to move beyond the present conditions and attain ever-greater grasp of the mystery of the self, which ultimately is the mystery of God. Thus our treatment of Lonergan will help us to move the integrative epistemology presented in this framework further than what we were able to do with Kegan's theory.

7. LONERGAN: VIEWPOINTS AND HORIZONS

We concluded the second chapter with a discussion of self-transcendence of the subject that is achieved through self-appropriation at various levels, particularly through the multi-dimensional reality of meaning. Through the evolution and construction of meaning, the subject achieves self-transcendence at the conscious and intentional operations. In chapter two, we emphasized the fact that meaning is not something static, but rather dynamic. The subject is constantly pushing forward and beyond the present boundaries. We detect this dynamism in Lonergan's notion of the subject even in *Insight*, for he insists in the preface to the book that the whole work was written from a moving viewpoint.[196] And as David Tracy explains, "Each context is set up only to reveal by the very dynamism of the questions that it raises but cannot answer the need for a 'higher view point.' Thus, the entire movement of *Insight* itself is the development of context leading to context until all contexts lead to a deeper, structured, and at its final stage, self-affirmed recognition of the unrestricted desire to know as the moving view point behind and grounding all explicit scientific, philosophic and theological ideals."[197] What Tracy has to say here has significant bearing on what the later Lonergan does in regard to these moving, higher view points.

In his later works, Lonergan no longer talks about 'a moving viewpoint.' He introduces another term that becomes crucial to his furthering the notion of the subject's self-transcendence. And that term is 'horizon.' Horizon becomes so crucial to Lonergan that Tracy in his book *The Achievement of Bernard Lonergan*[198] states that his objective in that work is "to expose the method of horizon-analysis employed by Bernard Lonergan."[199]

Walter Conn attempts to clarify Lonergan's earlier use of 'world' and 'context' in *Insight* (1956), "Metaphysics of Horizon" (1963) and *Method in Theology* (1972). This is what he has to say:

The exact relationship between 'world' and 'horizon' in Lonergan's writings is not easy to determine. Both the terms are fairly recent [Conn wrote this 1981]. *Insight* used 'viewpoints' and 'contexts' which seemed to relate to each other as the later 'subject-pole' and 'object-pole' of horizon as discussed in "Metaphysics of Horizon" (1963). In relation to this version of horizon, the subject's world (*existenz* and *aggiornomento* 1964) appears to constitute the 'object-pole' (still 'world') which is structurally related to a subject-pole now called 'standpoint' of the subject. Actually the 1963 and 1972 versions seem fundamentally the same insofar as both are rooted in the same image; but the "Metaphysics of Horizon" begins with horizon as a 'maximum field of vision from a determinate standpoint,' it very quickly turns horizon into a somewhat vague 'umbrella' that covers both subjective and objective poles, thus confusing at least the literal image, if not the metaphysical meaning. 'Horizon' and 'world' then, now seem to be practically equivalents, perhaps for the sake of theoretical distinction, we may say that a subject's world is defined by and lies within the boundary of his or her horizon, both of which refer to the object-pole correlative to the subject's standpoint.[200]

Reading Lonergan's later works, we can say that horizon connotes the world of meanings in which the subject operates and against which backdrop the subject explores future possibilities of transcendence. In the words of Lonergan, "In its literal sense the word, horizon, denotes the bounding circle, the line at which earth and sky appear to meet. This line is the limit of one's field of vision. As one moves about, it recedes in front and closes in behind so that, for different standpoints, there are different horizons."[201] Michael Novak's writes of horizons in a similar vein, "horizon indicates a dynamic orientation, for the human subject is not stationary. He moves through many and varied experiences, gains new insights, sometimes is led by experiences to shift those criteria of relevance and evidence that guide his judgment, and regularly 'tries to do' projects that carry his view into the future."[202] Horizons are rooted in the past and oriented toward the future.

In the context of this study, horizons for Lonergan are "the structured resultant of past achievement and, as well, both the condition and the limitation of further development. They are structured. All learning is, not a mere addition to previous learning, but rather as organic growth out of it."[203] Horizons are crucial to the understanding of finitude and self-transcendence. They, in fact, encompass our knowledge, our attitudes, our values, and our Ultimate meaning and value, God. "Horizons then are the sweep of our interests and of our knowledge; they are the fertile source of further knowledge and care; but they are also the boundaries that limit our capacities for assimilating more than we already have attained."[204] Horizons are the parameters of our finitude and the backdrop for transcendence. Within the horizon lies what we know and love; beyond the horizon lies what draws us to constantly transcend present knowledge and love.

7.1 PIAGET'S INFLUENCE ON LONERGAN IN THE FORMULATION OF HORIZONS

We have referred to the influence of psychology and psychologists on Lonergan. Here, "it should not be difficult to notice in Lonergan's formulation of horizon an influence from Piaget's understanding of the relationship between the individual to the environment in terms of the adaptive processes of assimilation and accommodation."[205] The progression and dynamism of the radical shifts in horizon that we see in Lonergan evidently reflects Kegan's onward and upward moving stage theory.

Consistent with Lonergan's heuristic process of pushing from the known to the unknown, one must be aware that what lies beyond one's horizon consists not principally of answers but of questions that are as yet unanswered. In Tracy's words, "I cannot have any clear picture of either the boundary or the limitations of my present horizon until, as a matter of fact, I have already surpassed it. Its boundaries are obscure and hazy to me. And what is outside it I simply cannot see."[206] The subject is constantly drawn to the realms of the unknown and in the process the subject self-transcends.

It is significant that when talking about horizons, Lonergan uses language that would be characteristic of a developmental psychologist. Of horizons he writes, "They [horizons] are related as successive stages in some process of development. Each later stage presupposes earlier stages, partly to include them and partly to transform them."[207] What are these successive stages he is referring to? They are intellectual, moral and religious conversions. Much in the line of stage theorists, Lonergan speaks of the relationship between horizons as one of sublation to which we will return in the section on conversion.

8. CONVERSION

Lonergan takes the normal understanding of conversion as *metanoia* and brings it into the arena of horizon-analysis:

> It is not merely a change or even a development; rather, it is a radical transformation on which follows, on all levels of living, an interlocked series of changes and developments. What had been of no concern becomes a matter of high import. So great a change in one's apprehensions, and one's values accompanies no less a change in oneself, in one's relations to other persons, and in one's relations to God.[208]

A conversion is a radical shift in horizon, whether it is intellectual, moral or religious.[209] Lonergan uses Joseph de Finance's distinction between horizontal and vertical exercises of freedom to clarify what a conversion is:

> A horizontal exercise is a decision or choice that occurs within an established horizon. A vertical exercise is the set of judgments and decisions by which we move from one horizon to another. Now there may be a sequence of such vertical exercises of freedom, and in each case the new horizon, though notably deeper and broader and richer, none the less is consonant with the old and a development out of its potentialities. But it is also possible that the movement into a new horizon involves an about-face; it comes out of the old by repudiating characteristic features; it begins a new sequence that can keep revealing ever greater depth and

breadth and wealth. Such an about-face and new beginning is what is meant by a conversion.[210]

Conversion, in as far as it brings about the radical movement from one horizon to another, is a process of self-transcendence.[211] In fact, each conversion is a modality, a fundamental form of self-transcendence.[212] It is the particular mode of achieving and realizing transcendence.

For Lonergan, conversion is ontic. It is not something that happens to someone. It is a state to which one is transformed. That state is not one of inactivity, but of dynamism. The transformation of horizon is so real that s/he apprehends differently, values differently, relates differently. The convert is changed as a knower, as a conscious and intentional operator, as a self-transcending subject.

8.1. Intellectual Conversion

The first of the conversions that Lonergan deals with is intellectual conversion. Tracy affirms that "cognitive transcendence can accurately be named 'intellectual conversion.'"[213] However, one needs to be cautious when speaking of intellectual conversion. It cannot be confused with an acquisition of new knowledge, however enormous it may be. We cannot talk of intellectual conversion unless there is a radical shift in horizon. Previous misconceptions and myths have to be eliminated and discarded. The subject needs to see reality in a totally different light. Lonergan writes, "intellectual conversion is a radical clarification and, consequently, the elimination of an exceedingly stubborn and misleading myth concerning reality, objectivity, and human knowledge."[214]

Lonergan brings more clarity to what he means by intellectual conversion when he writes,

As soon as they [Lonergan is referring to those whom he calls naïve realists, empiricists and idealists] begin to speak of knowing, of objectivity, of reality, there crops up the assumption that all knowing must be something looking. To be liberated from the blunder, to discover the self-transcendence proper to the human process of coming to know, is to break often long-ingrained habits of thought and speech. It is to acquire the mastery in one's own house that is to be had only when one knows precisely what one is doing when one is knowing. It is a conversion, a new beginning, a fresh start. It opens the way to ever further clarifications and developments.[215]

Intellectual conversion is really a process of conversion, and not merely a significant development in one's cognitive capacity. The person who experiences intellectual conversion has shifted from one horizon to another, which is radically different. In commenting on Lonergan's intellectual conversion, Tracy has this to say,

> It [intellectual conversion] is genuinely a conversion and not merely a development for it demands a radical turn away from what is experienced or sensed or imagined or conceived to what is rationally affirmed to be true. And that possibility, in its turn, demands a radical reorientation of the authentic subject from some little world of his own (more than likely, some dubious combination of animal faith and human error) to a world of intelligently understood and reasonably affirmed. It involves, in essence, the transformation of the subject from a horizon defined by its own psychological, sociological and cultural desires, fears and achievements to one that is accurately named a basic horizon, i.e., to the intelligent, the true, the good; indeed even the holy.[216]

Lonergan insists that intellectual conversion must always precede the other conversions. Richard Liddy commenting on this writes, "The reason for this order of exposition, I surmise, is that intellectual conversion is the origin of the categories necessary to *explain* the dynamics of religious and moral conversion."[217]

8.2. Moral Conversion

Intellectual conversion is rooted in the self-transcending subject's desire to know. However, this desire to know and the achievement of knowledge are not the end points. As Conn comments, "There is more. Our knowing is oriented toward action: we desire to know because we desire to act, and act intelligently. Our experiencing, understanding, and judging are directed not just to what is, but to what is to be done, not just to knowing reality, but to creating reality, and creating ourselves in the process."[218] In intellectual conversion, the intelligent subject achieves self-transcendence through a process of understanding, reflecting and judging. Then, "the rational subject, having achieved knowledge of what is and could be, rationally gives way to conscious freedom and conscientious responsibility."[219] Understanding of self and of reality has to lead one to action and responsibility in action. When this radical shift in horizon[220] occurs, then, we are dealing with moral conversion.

Although moral conversion is distinct from intellectual conversion, the two are closely related. "The radical dynamism of our spirit which manifested itself cognitively as a search for meaning and a demand for evidence now reveals itself on the level of moral consciousness as a quest for value and an insistence coming from within us on self-consistency in knowing and doing."[221] Conn expounds the same view in his books, *Conscience: Development and Self-Transcendence* and *Christian Conversion: A Developmental Interpretation of Autonomy and Surrender.*

We find that Lonergan returned to the theme of conversion in his later writings and gave it a remarkably significant role in his philosophy and theology. This sometimes misleads students of Lonergan to think that the whole notion of conversion was a later discovery for Lonergan. The term 'conversion' may not occur frequently in his earlier works, but the following from *Insight* should leave no doubt that the notion of conversion,[222] (moral conversion, in this instance) was already present there:

> The detached, disinterested, unrestricted desire to know grasps intelligently and affirms reasonably not only the facts of the universe of being but also its practical possibilities. Such practical possibilities include intelligent transformations not only of the environment in which man lives, but also of man's own spontaneous living. For that living exhibits an otherwise coincidental manifold into which man can introduce

a higher system by his own understanding of himself and his own deliberate choices. So it is that the detached and disinterested desire extends its sphere of influence from the field of cognitional activities through the field of knowledge into the field of deliberate human acts. So it is that the empirically, intelligently, rationally conscious subject of self-affirmation becomes a morally self-conscious subject. Man is not a knower but also a doer; the same intelligent and rational consciousness grounds the doing as well as the knowing; and from the identity of consciousness springs inevitably an exigence for self-consistency in knowing and doing.[223]

It is equally true that as Richard Liddy has pointed out, Lonergan's focus on human values, existential decision-making and historical scholarship that he exhibits in *Method in Theology* finds a new breakthrough in his thinking. Lonergan expresses this in a different language, the language of horizon and conversion. Liddy writes, "In that work [*Method in Theology*], his treatment of religious and moral conversion in history, far from 'dwarfing' his earlier work on intellectual conversion, only brings that work to 'a far fuller realization.'"[224]

In intellectual conversion, the self-transcending subject is in the arena of knowing; in moral conversion, s/he is in the realm of doing. In the former, the subject through self-appropriation is involved with facts of value, in the latter, the subject as the originator and existential does of these values. "Moral conversion is the radical change in the criterion of one's decisions and choices from satisfactions to values. It involves the thrust of our human freedom toward authenticity."[225] Experiencing, understanding, and judging must necessarily lead to reflection and critical reflection, which in turn moves one to act and act responsibly. Conn expresses Lonergan's presentation of moral conversion thus: "In its full sense, moral conversion is the performance not just as discovery, recognition, affirmation of one's moral consciousness in all its implications, but also and especially as the active decisive decision to accept fully the exigence of that moral consciousness, the existential choice of oneself as a free and responsible originator of value of one's judgments, decisions, and choices."[226]

We need to make just one comment about affective conversion. It is unclear if Lonergan sees this as being separate from the other three conversions[227] he constantly talked about. One thing is sure that Lonergan had made a major shift from the cognitive mode of approach evident in his early works, including *Insight* to the discussions of meaning, value, and especially the importance of the psychology and experience of love that affects the human person and drives him or her to the various modalities of self-transcendence. One thing seems to be clear that the desire for self-transcendence which is essential to intellectual, moral, and religious transcendence are passionate and involved, and to that extent each of them can be spoken of as affective conversions.

8.3. Religious Conversion

Lonergan has given a brief but insightful treatment of religious conversion in *Method in Theology*: "Religious conversion is being grasped by ultimate concern. It is other-worldly falling in love. It is total and permanent self-surrender, not as an act, but as a dynamic state that is prior to and principle of subsequent acts."[228] We notice that Lonergan uses the words, 'being grasped of ultimate concern' which is very reminiscent of Paul Tillich. However, he moves to use a much more personalistic analogy, that of falling in love. He takes empirical experience of falling in love—an experience that is dynamic and dramatic and uses it an analogy for explaining religious conversion as other-worldly falling in love.

The drive for self-transcendence that remains in this world alone is bound to be frustrated. Self-transcendence is the drive to, the pull towards, the attraction of, and the captivation with the Transcendent. As Conn says, "In this transformation [moral conversion] we realize that personal development is only partially self-creation; it is also, and centrally, a radical gift. The fullness of this transformation, and therefore of its power, lies in religious conversion."[229] Lonergan uses the traditional theological terms, operative and cooperative grace, to explain religious conversions:

> Operative grace is the replacement of the heart of stone by a heart of flesh, a replacement beyond the horizon of the heart of stone. Cooperative grace is the heart of flesh becoming effective good works through human freedom. Operative grace is religious conversion. Cooperative grace is the effectiveness of conversion, the gradual movement toward a full and complete transformation of the whole of one's living and feeling, one's thoughts, words, deeds, and omissions.[230]

Religious conversion in the Christian context is God's love flooding our hearts through the grace of the Holy Spirit.[231]

It is necessary to draw attention to Lonergan's insistence that religious conversion is "total and permanent self-surrender without conditions, qualifications, reservations."[232] This unrestricted self-giving is open-ended. The convert is potentially open to infinite possibilities is only a response to God's first act of Grace. God's generosity in letting humans participate in God's divinity and infinite possibilities.

8.4. Sublation

The kind of unrestricted self-giving we described in religious conversion fulfills the capacity for self-transcendence and is manifested in our limitless questions at every level of conscious and intentional operations and the various conversions.

> The mystery that we come upon when we keep pushing at our inquiry, reflection and deliberation is what comes into our hearts and prompts their utter response. When we are in love with God our constant going-beyond has engaged with a worthy beloved. We can keep going-beyond with God endlessly. There is always more light, life, and love to serve, admire, and desire.[233]

Religious conversation is foundational for the other two conversions. For Lonergan, it is "a total being-in-love as the efficacious ground of all self-transcendence, whether in the pursuit of truth or in the realization of human values or in the orientation man adopts to the universe, its ground, and its goal."[234]

We have seen that intellectual, moral, and religious conversions are all modalities of the same self-transcendence, the single pulsating drive that is part and parcel of human existence. The question is how are they related. Does moral conversion supercede intellectual conversion? Does religious conversion make moral conversion make intellectual and moral conversions obsolete? It should be obvious that Lonergan has taken pains to show the relatedness of these three modalities of transcendence that there can be no negation of the preceding conversions because one has progressed to the next modality.[235] As such, "it is possible, when all three occur within a single consciousness, to conceive their relations in terms of sublation."[236] Lonergan, provides us some clarification for the use of the term "sublation'.

> I would use this notion [sublation] in Karl Rahner's sense rather than Hegel's to mean that what sublates goes beyond what is sublated, introduces something new and distinct, puts everything on a new basis, yet so far from interfering with the sublated or destroying it, on the contrary needs it, includes it, preserves all its proper features and properties, and carries them forward to a fuller realization within a richer context.[237]

There is a danger to suppose that because religious conversion sublates moral conversion and moral conversion sublates intellectual conversion, at the order of occurrence the intellectual conversion always happens first and religious conversion last.[238] Lonergan says that actually it is the reverse, because God's gift of his love is antecedent to the other conversions.

The term sublation immediately takes us to Kegan's stages of ego-development and how when a higher stage has been reached nothing of what the person was in the previous stage is lost, but is integrated into the next stage with a richer context. In fact, what the subject had considered to be an object, something extraneous has become the subject, a part of one's identity. There is remarkable resemblance in the way Kegan and Lonergan present this notion.

9. CONCLUSION

That we are limited as humans and as creatures is part of our daily experience. However, there is a drive within the human spirit that is never tied down by the reality of human finitude. The exigence to self-transcendence is quintessential to being human. This human self-transcendence is not an elusive, ethereal substance within the human subject. It is to some extent empirical. We have seen this to be true in both Kegan and Lonergan. The psychological theory of Kegan gives us ample evidence to the fact of human self-transcendence. As a psychologist, he had to confine his inquiry to the empirical. However, we pointed out from Kegan's first publication *The Sweeter Welcome,* it would not be far fetched to connect the craving for greater and deeper meaning in human development (self-transcendence) with the experience of the Hasidic mystic who regards the secular and the profane as a preliminary stage of the holy.[239] Similarly, Lonergan in his exposition of self-transcendence began with the observable operations of experience, understanding, reflecting, and deciding. He moved them into the arena of the horizons and treated the conversions as modalities of self-transcendence. However, he presented all these modalities of self-transcendence as being "revealed in retrospect as an under-tow of existential consciousness, a dynamic state that is prior to and principle of the subsequent modalities.[240]

Part of next chapter will be devoted to searching for biblical and scriptural roots for the framework we have presented in the first four chapters.

CHAPTER V
HUMAN EXISTENCE: THE EVER-UNFOLDING MYSTERY
OF GRACE IN EXILE

1. INTRODUCTION: PARADOX OF FINITUDE WITH INFINITE POSSIBILITIES

This chapter will be comprised of three sections. In the first section, we will recapitulate what we have written in the previous four chapters. It will help us to recall the reason and purpose for the study. The second section will focus on the theological framework for doing Christian anthropology presented here. We will proceed to show that the suggested theological framework is not something novel. It has a long tradition in Christian thought. We will show that the early Greek Fathers of the Church present a Christian anthropology that is firmly grounded in the twin themes of the "image of God" and divinzation or deification. In these two themes we will see the source and destiny of what we have termed: the seemingly paradoxical experience of our finitude that harbors within itself infinite possibilities. The source of this paradoxical experience is God, since humans are created in God's image and the destiny of the humans is also God, we have been fashioned to be partakers of God's own divinity. Then, we will revisit the issues and challenges for contemporary Christian anthropology, which we presented in the first chapter. These are intended to point to future explorations of these issues and hence will not be done in great detail.

In the statement of the situation, we pointed out that Catholic theology had made significant progress in stepping out of the monolithic edifice built on a single system of thought, Scholastic philosophy. Catholic theologians have entered into conversation with contemporary philosophies of existentialism, phenomenology, Marxism, and a host of others to render Christian thinking and living more relevant to the twentieth century Christian. In the field of moral theology, some initial progress was made by freeing itself from minimalism and legalism that had to some extent sullied the otherwise rich Catholic moral tradition. This was in the immediate aftermath of Vatican II. However, in the last couple of decades we seem to have come to a watershed. One of the reasons for this, we said, was because Catholic moral theology has not been able to shake off the strong hold of faculty psychology. Even when theologians engage in a fruitful dialogue with contemporary psychology and regard the human subject as holistic, personal and developmental, the human person is not considered as a whole, but fragmented into body, soul, intellect and will. We suggested that this problem with Catholic moral theology is indicative of a larger problem. There is a real need for an alternate framework for doing Christian anthropology.

The second purpose of the work was to show how a fruitful dialogue between psychology and theology could benefit the theological enterprise. To this end we proposed to explore 'what it means to be human' in the works of psychologist Robert Kegan and theologian Bernard Lonergan. Our research led us to examine the notion of self-transcendence in Bernard Lonergan and Robert Kegan's theory of the human person as meaning-maker. Self-transcendence and meaning-making are crucial to their understanding of what it means to be human. For Lonergan, the human person realizes various levels of self-transcendence by a firmer grasp of the meaning of human existence through the dynamics of self-appropriation. For Kegan, to be human means to be a meaning-maker. And through meaning-making the human person achieves various levels of transcendence. We established that for both Lonergan and Kegan, there is a common integrative epistemology, the search for meaning. In both Lonergan and Kegan we discern what LeRon Shults calls "the creaturely nature of the search for meaning" and through this work we promote Shults' keen observation that "[t]he emergence of an integrative epistemology is evident in the growing dialogue between theology and natural sciences, which have developed conceptual frameworks to incorporate the current epistemological resolution."[241]

2. RECAPITULATION

In chapter one we introduced the basic question: What does it mean to be human?

We pointed out that this question receives multifarious answers from different disciplines of learning. The biologist and the geneticist have different answers from the sociologist and the cultural anthropologist. The physicist and the astronomer look at the meaning of being human from the perspective of the cosmos and the place of the human in the universe. The psychologist and the psychiatrist have perspectives on the human that may only tangentially meet those of the economist and the politician. The philosopher and the theologian are concerned with the ultimate origin, purpose and destiny of human existence. However, each is talking about the same reality: the human person. Each adds a crucial perspective to the better understanding of the seeming paradoxes and conundrums of human experience. It is in the best interest of each to learn from the others so that the mystery of the human person can be better fathomed and a more significant understanding of human existence can be worked out. A brief presentation of the thought of Max Scheler and Maurice Blondel seem to point to a positive and promising view of what it means to be human. We explored their contributions in this area and indicated a direction for working out a framework for contemporary Christian anthropology. The general outline of this framework was to regard the total openness that is intrinsic to being human as well as to behold the human as the meeting place of transcendence and immanence.

In chapter two, we elaborated the central notion of self-transcendence in Lonergan's theology. For Lonergan, the human subject realizes itself in an ever-progressive, ever-surpassing grasp of one's self through authentic self-transcendence. In other words, for Lonergan, the human subject cannot be understood apart from its intrinsic exigence to transcend one's present possibilities. The existential subject is Lonergan's starting point and this existential subject, through intentional and conscious operations, ever more fully realizes his/her self-transcending subjectivity through "the unfolding of a single thrust, the eros of the human spirit."[242] We walked through Lonergan's development as a thinker from his writings on Thomas, the Verbum articles, *Insight*, Halifax lectures, the three Collections and *Method in Theology* and his later works. We showed how Lonergan critiqued the empiricists, the rationalists, the idealists, Kant and Hegel and presented his solution to the problem of knowledge or understanding in the notion of self-appropriation. The act of understanding, for Lonergan, is the clue to understanding the human person. It is through self-appropriation that a human subject is capable of insight, which is basic to all knowledge and all human activity. Through self-appropriation, the subject transcends the world of subjects and objects and is capable of appropriating truth. Self-appropriation is the consciousness of oneself as the operator at all levels of operations. In Lonergan's words,

> "First of all, self-appropriation is advertence--advertence to oneself as experiencing, understanding, and judging. Secondly, it is understanding oneself as experiencing, understanding, and judging. Thirdly, it is affirming oneself as experiencing, understanding, and judging. The analysis of knowledge, then yields three elements: experience, understanding, judging."[243]

Through self-appropriation, one transcends the confines of one's own limitedness and reaches beyond oneself. Insight is the first instance of self-transcendence of the human subject. Lonergan describes various 'successive, related, but qualitatively different levels' at which a subject expands one's self-transcendence: sensual, intellectual, rational, and responsible. For Lonergan, self-transcendence is part of consciousness as well as of intentionality. The notion of self-transcendence is embedded in transcendental intentionality which connotes an *a priori* that goes beyond what lies within our horizon to the unknown whole or totality of which we are currently aware of only a part. There is an openness to infinite possibilities.

We noted that while Lonergan in his early writings was concerned about insight and understanding, his intellectual development had naturally led him to focus his attention on meaning and its importance in the human enterprise. In David Tracy's words, "Lonergan's involvement in historical consciousness forced him to shift his interest from an almost exclusive concern with scientific intelligibility to study the multidimensional character of meaning."[244] Lonergan maintained that the different modes of consciousness and intentionality gave rise to different realms of meaning.[245] It is indeed the activity of meaning-making that pushes the subject into these various horizons. Consequently, self-transcendence of the subject is intimately linked to meaning-making. In fact, it is the meaning-making subject who is self-transcendent.

In the third chapter, we explored the psychological theory of Robert Kegan and its underlying understanding of what it actually means to be human. For Kegan, to be human means to be a meaning-maker. In the process of making meaning, the human person evolves while attaining a greater grasp of him/herself. Thus, meaning-making or meaning-construction is not an end in itself. It is the dynamic process by which the human person continually unravels the mystery of who s/he is throughout one's life. For both Lonergan and Kegan, meaning and self-transcendence are intricately linked to their understanding of what it means to be human. Meaning is crucial to the realization of self-transcendence in Lonergan's notion of the human subject. In Kegan's theory, through meaning-construction, the human person transcends his/her grasp of who s/he is at each stage of ego development.

Both Lonergan and Kegan acknowledge their indebtedness to Jean Piaget and his genetic epistemology. In fact, both of them take Piaget's theory as the starting point for their own understanding of the human person. They find the progressive, hierarchical movement of the subject toward greater accommodation and assimilation of the environment as the basis for the realization of transcendence and greater grasp of the deeper meaning of the self. It must also be noted that Kegan, while calling himself a neo-Piagetian, insists that he has taken Piaget's theory far beyond what the originator had envisaged. Kegan's theory pushes the limits of the cognitive development of the person to a comprehensive development, which includes the affective, the social, and the moral development as well. Similarly, Lonergan, though indebted to Piaget, has used Piaget's theory and masterfully integrated it with his own understanding of the human person and his/her transcendence. Lonergan's notion of the subject, pushes the limits of Piaget's theory to encompass the sensual, the intellectual, the affective, the moral, the religious development. Lonergan, as we pointed out in chapter four, sees the progression of this transcendence in the way he presents conversion: intellectual, moral, and religious.

There is a holistic perspective in the understanding of what it means to be human that is evident in both Kegan and Lonergan. The instrument that Kegan developed to map out the evolution of the self "Subject-Object Interview" suggests an assumption of a dichotomy on the part of Kegan. This could not be farther from the truth, as Kegan holds that the polarities that subject and object suggest are *a posteriori*. Kegan holds that the self or the person is the prior context and that the subject and object are presented in a dialectical context in the self. The self is a unit, a whole. In each stage of Kegan's theory, the self accommodates and assimilates into the self what was regarded as the objective pole in the previous stage. Lonergan repeatedly insisted that self-transcendence is the single, vibrant dynamism that pushes the subject from the lower levels to the higher. There is a single thrust that unifies the subject. That pulse of life is self-transcendence.

In chapter three, we presented Kegan's stage theory of ego development, which he has aptly named "the Evolving Self." We showed how the human person possesses an underlying unity while s/he constantly evolves through various stages of development. The whole process of development takes place in the context of a "holding environment," in which the self experiences the continuity of who s/he is while acquiring a greater and deeper level of understanding of who s/he is. However, Kegan's theory also is founded on the basic human experience that in this "holding environment" or the embeddedness there is a constant experience of disembeddedness. In other words, while human beings long for security and safety, there is a desire to venture out into the unknown and in some sense risk the very security of the known and comfortable environment. It is a common human experience that we all yearn for inclusion and intimacy while we crave after autonomy and individuality. This dividedness that is basic to human experience is crucial to development in Kegan's theory.

In Kegan's theory, the infant at birth is considered to be at stage 0. This stage, the Incorporative stage, is characterized by a lack of subject-object differentiation. In fact, the infant at birth has no object to relate to. The infant is no more than a bundle of reflexes. It is in the transition from stage 0 to stage 1, the Impulsive stage that the self comes to differentiate the subjective self from the environment, the object. In the Impulsive stage, the self identifies with his/her impulses. The toddler, who as an infant was a bundle of reflexes, begins to differentiate the self from the reflexes. Instead of being a bundle of reflexes, the toddler has reflexes. The reflexes are not identified with the self; they have become an object to the self. For Kegan, the transformation from stage 0 to stage 1 as the birth of the object.

The transformation from stage 1 to stage 2 is, for Kegan, the birth of the role. The child, who had identified him/herself with his/her perceptions and impulses, distinguishes that these perceptions and impulses are not him/herself, but they can be regulated. They are not the self, but can be objectified. The child moves from the land of fantasy into the world of reality. Between the ages of five and seven, there is a distinct shift in the psychological and social world of the child. At the Imperial stage, the youngster begins to realize not only *that* I am, but also *who* I am. It is the stage when a self concept emerges. The youngster is no more merely acted upon, but has evolved into an agent with a sense of true autonomy. However, there emerges also an identification of the self with one's needs, wants, and interests. The adolescent seeks to define his/her identity. In the process, s/he is begins to recognize the need systems of others and accept or not accept others. This results in what psychologists term 'mutuality.' Kegan states that at this stage, the adolescent begins to "coordinate, or integrate, one need system with another, and in so doing, I bring into being that need-mediating reality which we refer to when we speak of mutuality."[246] At the Interpersonal stage, as the self image of the adolescent is still in formation, the self is not capable of intimacy or mature mutuality. In fact, as Selman had observed in his study, adolescents find their self-image and self-concept on what others think of them. It is more a group identity, an identity that is rooted in the atmosphere of the peer group. The adolescent could almost identify him/herself with his/her relationships. The transformation that takes place as one moves into the Institutional stage is that the individual recognizes that s/he is not his/her relationships, rather s/he has relationships. By Institution here Kegan does not mean a structure outside of the self. He means the personal system that the self constructs through auto-regulation. The self has evolved into a psychic institution all by itself. In the Institutional stage, the self regarded him/herself as the psychic organization. Through the transformation that takes place in the Interindividual stage, the self is no more the organization, rather the organizer who constructs the organization. There is a distinct self who can enter into communion with other distinct selves. We can assert that there is an individuality that is differentiated enough to bring about an interindividuality.

At each stage of development, the ego transcends the previous grasp of the self. There is an ever-widening, ever-deepening understading of one's humanity. The developmental theory that Kegan propounds clearly espouses the intrinsic self-transcendence of the human person. At each stage, the self through a process of meaning-construction integrates what s/he regarded as the objective pole into a transformed self. At each stage, the evolving self is not negating who s/he is, but giving a radically fresh understanding of who s/he is. Even as meaning-making is integral to being human, so also self-transcendence is the essence of each one's humanity.

The fourth chapter served three explicit purposes. First, we established the link between Lonergan's notion of self-transcendence and Kegan's understanding of meaning. At first blush, meaning and self-transcendence might appear as two unrelated areas of human existence. We argued that the two are interrelated and in their complementarity, they open new vistas for a more relevant Christian anthropology. Kegan's constructive developmental theory of the Evolving Self rests on meaning construction of the self that flows into the evolving of the self in successive and ever greater growth of the already present self. The emphasis, of course, is on meaning and meaning-construction. However, this can hardly be understood without the assumption that the present self is capable of a successive, progressively higher and greater meaning of the self. Hence, meaning in Kegan's theory is deeply rooted in self-transcendence. On the other hand, Lonergan's notion of self-transcendence is possible only because the subject constantly seeks meaning through a heuristic process of transcendental questions to move the subject from the world of known meaning, horizons and conversions to those that are as yet unknown. Without meaning, that single thrust pulsating through life would be frustrated. Meaning is so crucial to Lonergan's notion of self-transcendence that, as David Tracy has pointed out, Lonergan had necessarily to shift from his exclusive interest in insight in his earlier writings to the study of the multidimentional character of meaning.[247] Meaning and self-transcendence are intricately and intimately linked. Kegan and Lonergan approached them from two different perspectives because of their own intellectual background and the disciplines to which they were wedded. While Kegan sees meaning-making as the warp and woof of what it means to be human, it is evident that this meaning-making results in self-transcendence that makes the evolving of the self possible.

The second purpose of chapter four was to explicitate what Kegan as a psychologist could not do, viz., to ask the metaphysical question the why and wherefore of transcendence that is part and parcel of being human. In order to do this, we turned to Kegan's first published work *The Sweeter Welcome*. This book comes from the very heart of the author. It gives us a clear indication as to what Kegan holds as the meaning, source and destiny of human existence. As Kegan wrote this book, not as a psychologist, but as someone captivated by Hasidic mysticism and its approach to the mystery of human existence, he was offended by the nihilism of Nietzsche and Sartre. Humans, for Sartre, are strangers to each other; they are condemned to nothingness and meaninglessness, and human existence is utter absurdity. Humanity was bereft of the life-giving mystery of the Beyond. Nihilists had exiled the transcendence of the human spirit. Kegan was equally disturbed by what Kegan calls "the accommodationist approach" of

Camus, who had concluded that though human life may be absurd, it is not meaningless or unsatisfying. Kegan offers his approach to the mystery of human existence. When confronted by the Nihilists' denial of anything transcendent about the human spirit, Kegan's staunch reply is: human existence is an immersion in transcendence. In Kegan's own words, "We may be living without the vertical. We may live on the horizontal. But the horizontal is the holy."[248] In propounding this approach, Kegan is, in fact, echoing the spirituality of Neo-Hasidism, especially as expounded in the philosophy of Martin Buber. Kegan achieves his aim masterfully by deftly drawing insights from some of the literary works of Saul Bellow and Bernard Malamud. Kegan speaks loud and clear through his book, *The Sweeter Welcome*, that the immanent and the transcendent are married in the human experience. The two are not dichotomous, for indeed the beyond is within us. We proceeded to show the underlying implication of the transcendence-in-immanence for Kegan's psychological theory of the Evolving Self. According to Kegan's theory of the Evolving Self, the human person is a meaning-maker and through the process of meaning-making, s/he evolves from the lower stages of development to the higher in a spiraling, forward-moving, ever-progressive movement. The person does not change into another, but holds on to the same personal identity while constantly gaining a greater and deeper grasp of the transcending mystery of one's humanity.

The third purpose of chapter four was to further develop Lonergan's notion of the subject as self-transcendent. Chapter two had traced Lonergan's own intellectual development of the notion of the subject as self-transcendent and how self-transcendence is crucial to understanding the human person. However, we limited ourselves to exploring the subject's self-transcendence through conscious and intentional operations. We also explored the importance of meaning to self-transcendence. In the fourth chapter, we showed how Lonergan in his later years, influenced by phenomenology and a historical consciousness, began to focus his attention on horizon, which is the totality of the subject's world of meaning that is currently limited by the extent of one's past knowledge and caring and yet tending to push the limits farther and farther. "Horizon indicates a dynamic orientation, for the human subject is not stationary. He moves through many and varied experiences, gains new insights, sometimes is led by experience to shift those criteria of relevance and evidence that guide his judgment, and regularly 'tries to do' projects that carry his view into the future."[249] This led us into the discussion of Lonergan's understanding of conversion, which he considered a radical shift of a subject's horizon, whether it is intellectual, moral, affective, or religious.

3.   RETRIEVING THE TRADITION OF IMAGO DEI/THEOSIS

The framework for Christian anthropology presented in this work has been built on an integrating epistemology that we have seen in both Lonergan and Kegan. Their strong emphasis on the integrating rather than the dichotomizing experiences in human existence led us to stress underlying notion of human self-transcendence. In this section we want to show that the theology of *imago dei* and *theosis* provides us with a theological tradition to strengthen our framework. Our framework is to be seen as a way of retrieving and enriching the *imago dei/theosis* tradition.

4.   IMAGO DEI: SEARCHING THE SCRIPTURES

The framework for doing Christian anthropology proposed here is not something new or novel. It is rooted in the twin biblical and theological notions of *imago Dei* and divine participation or *theosis*. Though it is beyond our scope to do an in-depth scriptural and theological treatment of these two topics, it is important we provide some insights into them.

We have said that the central concern in Christian anthropology is to explore the answer to the question, 'what does it mean to be a human?' The very first chapter of the book of Genesis states, "So God created man in his own image, in the image of God he created him; male and female he created them." (Gen 1:27) This is the biblical foundation for understanding what it means to be human. This is a profound theological as well as an anthropological statement. It says as much about humans as it does about God. It assures us that the starting point for understanding what it means to be human is to explore the height and depth, the length and width of the meaning of the notion of image of God.

The Hebrew Scriptures and the Christian Scriptures take the notion of humans created in God's image as a given. There are several explicit references to this notion in both the sources: Gen 1:26-28; Gen 5:1-3; Gen 9:5-6; Heb 1:3; James 3:9; Rom 8:29; 2 Cor 3:18; 2 Cor 4:4; Col 1:15; Col 3:10. There seems to be an acceptance of this notion in the Hebrew Scriptures[250] that there is no attempt to develop a systematic treatment of the notion of the image of God in the bible. However, it is safe to say that the Hebrew Scriptures present all humankind as being in some way like God. The image of God is seen as being universal. As we shall see later, the Greek Fathers would draw fine distinctions between the terms 'image' and 'likeness'. The Christian Scriptures build on the Hebrew understanding of the image of God, but place heavy emphasis on the divine purpose and its embodiment in the person who believes in and is united with Christ. As Melinda Johanning puts it, "The Old Testament presents man [sic] made in the image of God whereas the New Testament proclaims Christ to be the image of God with man [sic] predestined to be conformed to the image."[251] Paul presents Christ as "the image of the invisible God." (Col 1:15) and humans to have been fashioned in the image of the Image of God. The purpose of Christian life is "to be conformed to the image of Christ Jesus". (Rom 8:29). Pauline anthropology is rooted in Christology. Exploring the image of God from its intimate connection with Christ lends itself to a vibrant Christian anthropology. However, as noted earlier, there is no systematic development of the image of God in the Scriptures. We need to turn to the Eastern Fathers of the Church to provide us insights into this biblical notion of the image of God.

5. IMAGE OF GOD IN THE GREEK FATHERS OF THE CHURCH

The theology of image is far better developed in the Greek Fathers than among the Latin Fathers. Lot-Borodine opines that the reason for this is because the Greek theologians speculated less and insisted more than Latin theologians on the image of God imprinted on the human soul.[252] While the Western Church seems to prefer formulas in dry and abstract expressions, the Eastern thinkers use their imagination and poetic intuition to speak of the reality of the human in relation to God in their articulation of the image of God theology.

Melinda Johanning points out that "the patristic conception of the image of God in man [sic] is of uncommon significance for historical theology since at times it almost commands the entire view of man held by the Fathers."[253] She also asserts that the Greek Fathers employ the image of God as their centerpiece of Christian teaching about humanity. George Maloney concurs with this view, "The simple words image and likeness (*eikon* and *omoiosis*) provided the early Christian writers with an analogy around which they developed their best theological thought on Christology, the Trinity, creation and grace, the problem of nature and supernature, the laws of the spiritual life and its development and progress."[254]

It appears that the first one to combine Jewish and Greek thought on the image theme was Philo, the Alexandrian Jew. He accomplished this integration without sacrificing or destroying the Old Testament understanding of God. Johanning puts it this way:

> Philo's presentation is influenced by strains, which pour in from Heraclitus, Anaxagoras, Socrates, Plato, and the Stoics, in the form of an immanent Being in the world, the transcendence of God, intermediaries, and divinization. Philo made modifications from the prevalent pantheistic Logos doctrine to fit his theistic system. His Logos is not identical with God but mediates between Him and the world.[255]

Philo's influence on the Greek Fathers is clear. According to Johanning, "On various levels, one is not surprised to find that Alexandrian orientation finds its springboard in Philo."[256] We will proceed to look at some of the key Greek Fathers who developed the theology of the image of God.

5.1. St. Irenaeus of Lyons

The first Christian writer who used the image of God as a framework to integrate his theological presentation of Christianity was Irenaeus of Lyons. His main concern as a bishop was pastoral. He wanted to combat the Gnostic heresy. He wrote *Adversus Haereses* to demonstrate the falsity inherent in maintaining the duality between matter and spirit. Therefore, it must be kept in mind that his goal was not to develop a complete doctrine of the image of God, but to show the universality of God's salvific plan. This in no way minimizes his influence on those who came after him. The way he described the image of God notion had significant influence on Christian writers of the East.

For Irenaeus, in order to understand what humanity means, we must go back to the first man, Adam, who was created according to the image of Jesus Christ, the God-man. God the Creator molded the human according to the pattern of the Divine Logos. Irenaeus repeatedly asserts that the prototype for humanity is Jesus and every human person is destined to be like the prototype. To be fully human is to be more and more like Jesus. George Maloney outlines Irenaeus' thinking thus:

> Adam was born an image of the Image, Jesus Christ, in possessing a human, material body and a soul with the knowing and willing faculties that allowed him to know God and His will and love Him by obeying. The likeness he possessed in an embryonic form, susceptible to increasing growth as the first man cooperated with the two hands of God, the Logos and the Holy Spirit, in doing the will of the Creator. He was a child (*pais* in Greek) as far as this Divine Life was developed. He was destined to move to greater maturity, to spiritual adulthood as he cooperated with the Divine Energies working in his person, not in his soul nor in his body as in distinct and separated parts, but these essential, component parts making up a total personal being.[257]

It is evident that for Irenaeus, the image of God is clearly rooted in his Christology and his Trinitarian theology. The notion that humans are created in the image of the Image (Logos) of God is a recurrent theme in the Greek Fathers. The place of the Holy Spirit in human effort as sanctification and return to the holiness of the prototype, who is both model and exemplar for human living, is crucial to the understanding of how humans can become fully human.[258] Maloney paraphrases the thinking of Irenaeus on the Christological and Trinitarian basis of the image of God theology thus:

> It is the Holy Spirit that finds man the gift of spiritual child-likeness; that is, that makes him a child to the likeness of the natural Son of God, the Logos, who is not only the model and exemplar of man's image but also of his likeness...God gives His Holy Spirit thorough the Logos in an act of continuous creation throughout greater growth in the spirit.[259]

There is a certain lack of clarity in Irenaeus as to how he understood the 'image' (*eikon*) and 'likeness' (*omoiosis*) in Genesis 1:26. In most of his writings, he does not make any distinction between the two. However, when he writes about the fall, Irenaeus makes a distinction between these two terms.[260] He teaches that Adam had lost his gift of life on account of the fall. Though he still possessed physical life, he had become corruptible and dead as regards his life in God. He had lost his 'likeness' to God though he still remained the image of God. This is an important distinction, not only for the later Greek Fathers, but also to the way we have presented being human in this work. Humans never lose the image of God but tarnish or mar the likeness to God through sin.

5.2. Origen[261]

Origen made unique contribution to the image of God theology. However, in his teaching he was deeply influenced by the Gnostic emphasis on the absolute immateriality of God. God, being pure spirit, could not take on elements of corporeality. Origen struggled to reconcile God's absolute transcendence and the Incarnation. He took the idea of the Logos from Greek philosophy as the communicator of God's goodness. Origen's concern was to show that though Jesus was God, he was nevertheless not the Father. We must bear in mind that the Church at this time was in the grip of Christological and Trinitarian controversies. Origen wrote of the Father as being the fountain of Godhead and yet maintained the divinity of the Son. There is at least implied Subordinationism in Origen's thought.[262] However, as Maloney points out, when it came to his theology and asceticism, Origen centered it "around the image and likeness of God in man with a thoroughness and consistency unknown in the writers before him."[263]   Like Irenaeus and Clement of Alexandria, Origen fashioned his anthropology around the Divine Logos as the revealer of divine knowledge.   Maloney explains that Origen's view was that the Divine Logos is the perfect and immediate Image of God, being of the same substance with the Father while humans are an imperfect and mediate image of God.   Humans are created 'according to the image' that is, immediately modeled on the Logos, Jesus Christ, and only mediately, through the intermediacy of the Logos, created according to the Image that is God the Father.[264]   In comparison to Irenaeus, Origen drew sharper distinction between 'image' and 'likeness'.   Origen held that Adam possessed both image and likeness. However, by the fall, Adam lost his privileges.

5.3. St. Athanasius of Alexandria

The Father of the Church who is credited with a singular contribution to the direction during the Christological controversy is St. Athanasius. Maloney says that "St. Athanasius stood out as a shining beacon of orthodoxy."[265] He felt called to defend the faith against the erroneous doctrine of Arianism. Athanasius, in contrast to Origen, staunchly held that Jesus Christ possessed full divinity. His basic thinking is

> If the Son is the perfect Image of the Father, He must be the same nature as the Father... If the Son is the Image of the Father and hence mirrors forth perfectly the same substance of the Father, it follows that whatever can be predicated of the Father can be also said of the Son. Athanasius follows this reasoning with the conclusion that the Son, being the Image of the Invisible God is also, qua image, invisible. The Logos-Image is eternal and transcendent, referring to the interior Trinitarian life. The Logos as Image of the Father is outside of a time-space relationship to His temporal incarnational mission.[266]

The originality of Athanasius is reflected in the way he distinguishes how Jesus is the Image of God while man is not in the image of God, but 'according to the image of God.' Maloney's summarization of the contribution of Athanasius has significant implications for the framework for doing Christian anthropology presented in this work. The possibility for finite humans to be oriented to seemingly infinite possibilities is rooted in the fact that, though we are creatures, we are created according to the transcendent God's own image. These ideas were expressed already by Irenaeus, Clement and Origen but it was Athanasius who first fixed the two terms, Image (eikon) as applicable to the Divine Logos and 'according to the Image' (*Kai'eikona*) as referring to human beings. Humans for Athanasius "are not themselves images' of God but are 'made after an image' that is, the Divine Son. The earlier writers applied image and 'according to the image' to as synonyms. Image for Athanasius now refers only to the Divine Son and implies the same substance with the Father. 'According to the Image' refers only to human beings and implies the participation of God's life through the instrumentality of Jesus Christ, the perfect Image.[267]

Athanasius also stressed that the image of God in humans is indestructible. In spite of the Fall and sin, the image of God is still alive in humans, though in a dimmed manner. Humans can restore the original likeness to God. However, humans of themselves are incapable doing it by themselves. It is only through the Divine Logos that there can be a rebirth through which humans can be 'according to His image.'[268]

6. THEOSIS: SEARCHING THE SCRIPTURES

The image of God theology logically led the Eastern Fathers to connect the origins of the humans to their destiny and goal. If we are created in God's own image and likeness, we are destined to participate in God's divinity. As Mark O'Keefe[269] explains the Eastern Fathers believed and taught that the goal and purpose of Christian life was to share or participate in the divine life. Two terms that are found recurrently in their writings are *theosis* and *theopoiesis*, which are translated as deification or divinization. Deification is not merely the destiny of the humans; it is also part of the process of living out one's daily Christian life. Hence, it is closely connected to the image of God theology we have just discussed. "It is precisely because human persons are created in the image of God that they are destined to participate in the divine life, that is, to be deified. *Theosis* is nothing other than the full and final realization of the creation of the human person in God's image."[270] Deification "has been understood to describe the sweep of Christian existence from creation in God's image to final union with God."[271]

The issue that scholars like G. W. Butterworth raise is that "there is nothing in either the Old or the New Testament which by itself could even faintly suggest that man might practice being a god in this world and actually become one in the next."[272] The suggestion here is that deification and participation in divinity are of a pagan origin that the early Church Fathers adopted and Christianized. Here, we must admit that the terms *theosis* and *theopoiesis* are not found in the Bible. However, there are some significant passages in both the Old and New Testament, especially in the New Testament that strongly suggest the theme of *theosis* and *theopoiesis*. If the Greek Fathers were greatly influenced by Hellenistic thinking, it must still be acknowledged that the Christian doctrine of deification is radically different from what the Hellenistic literature maintained. From this Keith Norman concludes that "since deification has a different content for the Fathers than for their pagan religious and philosophical counterparts, several scholars have seen the biblical influences as primary."[273] We have already shown how the theme of the image of God convinced the Fathers that humans are created in God's own resemblance. We highlighted that the *eikon* connotes the presence of the original in the image. Hence, the strongest argument for the doctrine of deification is rooted in the doctrine of the image of God.

Keith Norman points out that though throughout the Hebrew Scriptures Yahweh's sovereignty and transcendence is maintained without any shadow of a doubt, there are several instances where we find the epithet 'god' applied to men. He goes on to show that "I say, 'you are gods, sons of the Most High, all of you'" (Psalm 82:6) is by far the most prominent use of this term for the Christian doctrine of deification, because Jesus himself cites it in John 10: 34: "Is it not written in your law, 'I said you are gods?'" The early Church always taught that originally humans were created to be with God and were destined to be partakers of God's own nature. It was on account of the Fall that humanity was subject to sin and mortality. And it was the mission of Christ to help humans to fulfil that destiny. Paul's soteriology (Rom 2:7; 1 Cor 15:52; Eph 1:10; 2 Tim 1:10) and John's insistence[274] that we are heirs to divine sonship give enough basis to the Greek Fathers to develop the theology of *theosis*. We must make particular reference to 1 John 3:2: "Beloved, we are God's children now; it does not yet appear what we shall be, but we know that when he appears we shall be like him, for we shall see him as he is." There can be little doubt that the words 'we shall be like him' connote participation in God's own life.

O'Keefe contends that while several passages viz., Jn 17:21; 1 Cor 15:52; Eph 1:10; 2 Tim 1:10 allude to some aspect of *theosis*, it is the letter of 2 Peter 1:4 that explicitly speaks of "becoming partakers in the divine nature."[275] Keith Norman examines the same verse in the broader context of verses 3 to 15. He writes,

> The eschatological fulfillment of this promise (2 Peter 1:11) is similar to other New Testament passages which hold out the prospect of exaltation to the divine life. Hebrews 12:18-23 speaks of the city of God, the heavenly Jerusalem, and the company of apostles. 2 Timothy 2:12 promises a joint reign with Christ of we endure, while Revelation 1:6, 5:10 and 20:6 similarly describe the kingdom over which the saints will reign jointly with Christ in the age to come.[276]

7. THEOSIS IN THE GREEK FATHERS OF THE CHURCH

Before we look at what some of the leading Greek Fathers had to say about the theme of *theosis*, we should make some general remarks that are crucial to our discussion. The thinking of the Fathers in regard to divine participation is firmly rooted in their theology of the trinity and Christology. As we have pointed out earlier, the same is true of the way that the Fathers develop the theme of the image of God. As such, this becomes crucial for the framework for Christian anthropology presented in this study. "It is precisely because human persons are created in the image of God that they are destined to participate in the divine life, that is, to be deified."[277] To be created in the image of God, in the mind of the Fathers, is to be created in the image of triune God and in the image of Jesus, the image of the invisible God.

7.1. St. Irenaeus of Lyons

Irenaeus played an important role in preparing the way for later Greek Fathers to develop the theme of *theosis*, though he himself did not seem to use this word. Irenaeus presented the doctrine of the Incarnation "as the means of raising man [sic] to the level of divinity."[278] In the words of Irenaeus, "God became man in order that man might become God."[279] As noted earlier, in Irenaeus'·thought divine participation is consequent upon humans having been created in the image of God.[280] Norman expresses Irenaeus' thinking thus: "While only God himself is ingenerate and incorruptible by nature, the human soul was created not as a perfected god but as a being capable of unlimited progression towards godliness."[281]

The framework presented in this study has a remarkable resemblance to the anthropology expounded by Irenaeus. It is an optimistic and positive presentation of the human, created in God's own image, capable of being divinized through an openness to the infinite, God himself. In Norman's words, "By starting with an optimistic anthropology which emphasized man's [sic] likeness to God and unlimited potential, he [Irenaeus] was able to describe destiny in maturation as becoming a god without ceasing to be a man [sic]."[282]

7.2. Origen

Turning now to Origen, we see the same clear link between the image of God theology and his notion of *theosis* we saw in Irenaeus.[283] Like his predecessors, Irenaeus and Clement, Origen's notion of divine participation is through and through Trinitarian and Christological. Humans are created in the image of the triune God. The work of deification is the work of the Spirit to restore the image of God in Jesus, the divine Logos.

Like Irenaeus and Clement, Origen distinguished between *eikon* and *omioisis*. The latter was not given at creation except potentially; full resemblance and assimilation required moral and intellectual progress. 'The highest good, toward which all rational nature is progressing...is to become as far as possible like God.' [Norman's citation from Origen's *On First Principles*] It is the 'image' which gives man [sic] the capability of progressing to become like God; *omoiosis* is the fulfillment of that image.[284]

Incarnation, for Origen has direct bearing on deification of humanity. The *Logos* assumed both body and soul for the purpose of making it possible for humanity to progress to divinity. In Origen's own words the reason for the Incarnation was

> that from him there began that union of the divine with the human nature, in order that the human, by communion with the divine, might rise to be divine, not in Jesus alone, but in all those who not only believe, but enter upon the life which Jesus taught, and which elevates to friendship with God and communion with him every one who lives according to the precepts of Jesus.[285]

Origen makes the distinction that the *Logos* is God by participation in God Himself, while humans become gods by participation in the *Logos*. In the passage cited above, it is also clear that Origen emphasized human effort through the living of a moral life in imitation of the life of Christ as being necessary for anyone to make progress in the process of divinization. Johanning comments that for Origen both God and humans play important roles in the progression from image to likeness.[286] Divine participation is a gift from God. But nevertheless humans have to cooperate to be divinized.

7.3. St. Athanasius of Alexandria

When we come to Athanasius we see that he recurrently uses a verb form from the word, *theopoiein* or its cognate noun, *theopoiesis*, meaning, to deify or the work of divinizing.[287] Maloney points out that while Clement of Alexandria was the first to introduce this unbiblical term, "Athanasius canonized it as a synonym for the incarnational activity of the Word-made-flesh."[288]   Athanasius took the Incarnation as the key to his anthropology and consequently to his notion of *theosis*. Norman remarks that "Athanasius met the anthropological dilemma head-on with his soteriology, which forms the heart of his doctrinal system. Like Irenaeus, he centered his redemption theology on the Incarnation, which becomes the key to deification."[289]   Athanasius holds that by "taking on him what is ours he transforms us into what he is, that we, as incorporated and compacted and bound together in him through the likeness of the flesh may attain to a perfect man, and abide immortal and incorruptible."[290]   Athanasius reiterates the connection between the Incarnate Word and the deification of humanity in many of his writings.[291]

Athanasius, like his predecessors, sees an intimate connection between the Trinity and deification of humanity. "[Deification] becomes for Athanasius the vertebrae of a theological system of the Trinity's relationship with man [sic]."[292] In his treatise *Contra Arianos*, Athanasius writes,

> For therefore did He assume the body originate and human, that having renewed it as its Framer, He might deify it in Himself, and thus might introduce us all into the Kingdom of Heaven after His likeness. For man had not been deified if joined in a creature, unless the Son were very God; nor had man been brought into the Father's presence, unless He had been His natural and true Word who had put on the body.[293]

Though in the above passage there is no mention of the Holy Spirit, Athanasius does give a prominent role to the Spirit in the Christification and thus deification of humans. As Maloney puts it, "Athanasius uses the concept of man's divinization though Christ as a true synthetic principle in which also the divinizing activity of the Holy Spirit is clearly highlighted."[294]

The teaching of Irenaeus, Origen, and Athanasius on the image of God and divine participation provides a theological tradition for the framework for Christian anthropology presented in this study. The finitude which is part and parcel of human existence makes it clear to us that we are creatures totally dependent on God who is totally-the-other, the transcendent. However, out of God's goodness humans have been fashioned in his/her own image and likeness.

This is the spark of transcendence that has been infused into our inmost being. Due to our sinful human condition we do not reflect the image and likeness of God as we should. Through grace of the Holy Spirit and through human cooperation, we can resemble the image of God in Christ culminating in our final participation in God's own divinity. Johanning's summation of the theology of the Greek Fathers seems to reflect the position taken in this study:

> Greek Fathers often view the first created man as receiving the dignity of the image, with the fulfillment in the likeness to be reserved for the future. Man possesses power, a beginning of divinization, a call to the likeness, to be achieved through a gradual process of progressive actualization of perfection, in a potency to act relationship. In such progress, man becomes conformed to the Image, which is itself the Logos, through whom he is capable of comprehending and being united with the Incomprehensible God. Hence, man is a constantly changing position of progressive likeness to God. In such a process, the Logos (Son) and the Spirit play functional, pivotal, and causal roles.[295]

8. REVISITING ISSUES AND CHALLENGES FOR CONTEMPORARY CHRISTIAN ANTHROPLOGY

Before concluding, we must revisit the issues and challenges for any framework for Christian anthropology that we outlined in the first chapter. An elaborate and detailed appraisal of how the framework presented here adequately satisfies each of the six issues and challenges is not possible here. It is intended that in the future this framework could be explored in the light of these issues and challenges. For now, it must suffice to indicate that this framework, at first blush, takes the issues seriously and is, in a general sense, conscious of the challenges for contemporary Christian anthropology.

The framework presented here is an attempt to approach the question of what it means to be human from a perspective which takes human finitude as an unquestioned datum of experience while at the same time insisting that because humans are created in the image and likeness of God, we partake of God's own infinite possibilities. In this framework, there can be no dichotomy between the transcendent and the imminent because to be human is to be transcendence-in-immanence. Through the Incarnation Jesus has made it clear that grace is at home in nature. This framework highlights that nature and supernature are not to be taken as a two-tier reality, a multi-leveled notion. As humans we are "grace in exile"—not exile in a negative sense, but exiles who long for their home.

If the heart of what it means to be human is to live and enhance the image of God in us, there can be no substantial difference between male and female. It is true that the style or the manner in which the image of God is lived out and enhanced would be conditioned by gender just as it would be conditioned by history, culture, and individual personality. The polarization of the human into male and female and the ensuing power-play is, to say the least, minimized if our focus is the oneness in God's image. This framework can provide a corrective to the often one-sided anthropology that identifies human experience with the male experience. The human perspective, rather than the human as polarized in the male and the female, can inform the way we do Christian anthropology.

One of the objectives of this study was to provide an alternative to the predominant faculty psychology that still seems to hold a grip on Christian anthropology. Faculty psychology speaks about the body, the mind, the will, the soul, etc. The grave danger for Christian anthropology was to fragment the human into parts and forget the integrity and the unity of the person. Throughout this study, we have insisted that the human person is an integral whole. We have also emphasized the fact that this person, this integrated whole, is a dynamic self who in progressively transcending present possibilities enhances the mind, the heart, the will and the spirit, without in any way sabotaging the unity and integrity.

While enumerating the issues and challenges in the first chapter, we said that 'grace ultimately is God himself freely given or bestowed upon the whole of creation.'[296] We pointed out that there is a tendency to reify grace and speak of it as a thing that we can get or possess. In this framework, humanity and the whole of creation is the outpouring of God himself/herself. As images of God we are partakers of God's self. Grace is the pulsating thrust to constantly self-transcend. Grace, when reified, is rendered static, accidental, and a possession. In this framework, it has the possibility to be personal, dynamic and communitarian (Trinitarian).

If nature and supernature were not mutually exclusive in human experience, the next step would be to see whole of creation in this light. Separating humans from the rest of creation will be illogical. Having been created in God's image, humans will interact with the rest of creation as co-creators. Domination and destruction of God's creation will give place to enhancement and glorification of creation. There is a possibility here for a significant ecotheology.

One of the other challenges for Christian anthropology which we pointed out was that for the most part there was a misplaced emphasis in traditional eschatology on the *eschata* (the last things) rather than on the *eschaton* (Christ/God). We were more preoccupied with the temperature of hell and the geography of heaven than on God, the culmination and fulfillment of the desires of the human heart. This framework has found affirmation in the Greek Fathers who maintained that having been created in God's image we are destined to be partakers of God's divinity. Judgement, heaven, hell or purgatory should not distract us from our gaze on God, the Ultimate destiny of humans. *Imago Dei* and *theosis* are intimately linked to each other. We are created in God's image; we naturally crave and long to be one with God. The framework Christian anthropology presented here has rich potential for a meaningful rearticulation of Christian eschatology.

9. CONCLUSION

Lonergan's approach to what Vernon Gregson calls 'the desires of the human heart' provided us with an integrative epistemology for our framework. "The diversity of our enterprise is certainly real: the physician is not the tailor, the scholar is not the astronaut, the politician is not the chemist; but there is an underlying core in all our pursuits, and we do well to recognize it. The uncovering of that common core might encourage dialogue among the various sciences and between the humanities and the sciences."[297] Lonergan presented his notion of the subject in his/her integrity and unity. Although his notion of the subject entails operations, both conscious and intentional at various levels, Lonergan insisted that "the many levels of our consciousness are just successive stages in the unfolding of a single thrust, the eros of the human spirit."[298] This unifying single thrust is borne out in the progressive movement toward transcendence, intellectual, affective, moral, and religious.

Self-transcendence that is quintessential to Lonergan's notion of the subject has a psychological grounding and allowed us to see the parallel with Kegan's psychological theory of the 'Evolving Self.' Lonergan writes, "at the summit of the ascent from the initial bundle of needs and clamors and gratifications, there are to be found the deep-set joy and solid peace, the power and the vigor, of being in love with God. In the measure that that summit is reached, then the supreme value is God, and other values are God's expression of his love in this world, in its aspirations, and in its goals."[299]

Kegan's theory of the 'Evolving Self' has a certain resonance with Lonergan's notion of the self-transcending subject. The dynamic power of inquiry is at the root of Kegan's meaning-constructing self and Lonergan's notion of the subject. We saw how Kegan's stage theory shows the human person attaining higher levels of human existence through construction, deconstruction and reconstruction of the self. The underlying and unifying force for the whole theory was the dynamic power of inquiry. Self-transcendence, for Lonergan, is made possible because the human spirit is open to the infinite through the dynamic power of inquiry. This dynamic power of inquiry manifests itself in existential desires and longings: "the desires and longings which we have for what is beautiful, for what makes sense, for what is true, for what has value, and for what has ultimate value are at the heart of what it mean to be human."[300]

Kegan as a psychologist could deal only with the empirical at least as far as his theory is concerned. However, our excursus into his earlier work, *The Sweeter Welcome*, was instrumental in positing that the basis for the movement from lower to higher stages must point to the human longing for God. In the case of Lonergan the theologian, this thirst for God is very explicit. "The question of God, then, lies within man's horizon. Man's transcendental subjectivity is mutilated or abolished, unless he is stretching forth towards the intelligible, the unconditioned, the good of value. The reach, not of his attainment, but of his intending is unrestricted. There lies within his horizon a region for the divine, a shrine for ultimate holiness."[301] God is the ultimate desire of the human heart.

The twin themes of *imago Dei* and *theosis*, especially as developed in the theology of the Greek Fathers, provided a theological tradition that supports the framework for Christian anthropology developed here. Humans are created in God's image. The spark of divinity resides in every human heart. The openness to transcendence finds an explanation in *imago Dei*. The Fathers developed the doctrine of *imago Dei* in the context of the Trinity and Christology. Though this would have important repercussions for the framework for Christian anthropology, we could not engage in the needed discussion in this work. The doctrine of *theosis*, as developed by the Greek Fathers, was helpful in pointing out that not only the origin, but also the destiny of humans is to be found in God. Humans are made in God's image and are destined to be partakers of God's life.

Human finitude that is paradoxically open to infinite possibilities has its source and destiny in God. Humans created in the image of God experience themselves as immanence-in-transcendence. We are fully in agreement with Kegan when he maintains that at the heart of what it means to be human is a sense of being torn between embeddedness and disembeddedness. In Lonergan's view, the human subject is caught between the concreteness of limited existence and the exigence to self-transcendence. This exigence to self-transcendence is "united by the unfolding of a single transcendental intending of plural, interchangeable objectives"[302] which are realized through intellectual, moral, and religious conversions.

To be human, then, is to reflect the image of God. To reflect the image of God is to participate in the very life of God, unfolding the experience of the mystery of infinite openness to grace. The experience of grace, according to Lonergan, is "as large as the Christian experience of man's [sic] capacity for self-transcendence, of his unrestricted openness to the intelligible, the true, the good."[303]

NOTES

CHAPTER I: A FRAMEWORK FOR CHRISTIAN ANTHROPOLOGY

[1] David Tracy, *Blessed Rage for Order, the New Pluralism in Theology* (New York: Seabury Press, 1975); Claude Geffre, *Le Christianisme au risque de l'interpretation* (Paris: Cerf, 1983); its English translation *The Risk of Interpretation: On Being Faithful to the Christian Tradition in a non-Christian Age* (New York: Paulist Press, 1987); and *The Debate of Modernity*, eds. Claude Geffre and Jean-Pierre Jossua (London: SCM Press, 1992) would be representative of the new exploration.

[2] Vatican II, *Gaudium et Spes* (Pastoral Constitution on the Church in the Modern World), no. 62.in Austin Flannery, ed. *Vatican II: The Conciliar and Post Conciliar Documents* (Collegeville: Liturgical, 1975).

[3] We can draw attention to the works of Walter Kasper, Karl Rahner, Bernard Lonergan, Josef Fuchs, Bernard Haring, Gabirel Marcel, Jean-Luc Marion and a host of others.

[4] Representative works of these theologians are listed in the bibliography.

[5] Bernard Haring, *Free and Faithful: Moral Theology for Clergy and Laity* 3 vols (New York: Seabury Press, 1978).

[6] Josef Fuchs. *Human Values and Christian Morality*, tr. M.H. Heelan et al., (Dublin: Gill and McMillan, 1970).

[7] Enda McDonagh. *Doing the Truth: The Quest for Moral Theology*, Notre Dame, Ind.:University of Notre Dame, 1979 and Enda McDonagh *Moral Theology Renewed: Papers of the Maynooth Union Summer School 1964*, ed. Enda McDonagh, Dublin: Gill and Sons, 1965.

[8] Charles Curran. *Catholic Moral Theology in Dialogue*, Notre Dame, Ind.: Fides Publishers, 1982; Charles Curran._Moral Theology: A Continuing Journey*, Notre Dame, Ind.:University of Notre Dame Press, c. 1982 and Charles Curran. *Directions in Fundamental Moral Theology*, Notre Dame: University of Notre Dame Press, c. 1985.

[9] I do not draw attention to James Fowler and his commendable work in the area of faith development mainly because I am focusing on Catholic theologians who are engaged in mutual collaboration with psychology.

[10] Though the work is also an attempt to engage a theory of developmental psychology, viz., that of Robert Kegan and Bernard Lonergan's notion of self-transcendence, there is a significant difference between this study and that of Conn. Conn has explored the developmental theories of Jean Piaget, Lawrence Kohlberg, and Erik Erikson in the light of Lonergan's understanding of self-transcendence. Conn's interest is to study conscience. In his expanded study of conscience and conversion, in addition to the above mentioned developmental psychologists, he uses the work of Robert Kegan. Conn's focus is too narrow. Self-transcendence of the human subject cannot be limited to conscience or

conversion. The present study attempts to present the human subject as the locus of transcendence. Self-transcendence is intrinsic to being human. Self-transcendence permeates the whole human person and not just a part or a faculty.

[11] Maurice Blondel, L'action I quote Blondel's own words, "*Oui ou non, la vie humaine, a-t-elle un sens, l'homme, a-t-il une destine?*"

[12] Blondel had been captivated by the ideas of Leibniz and in fact, *Vinculum Substantiale* was based on the writings of Leibniz.

[13] John McNeil in his splendid book *The Blondelian Synthesis: A Study of the Influence of German Philosophical Sources on the Formulations of Blondel's Method and Thought* (Leiden: Brill, 1966) races Blondel's sources through Leibniz, Spinoza, and Kant. He also shows how Fichte's *Theory of Science* and Schelling's *Transcendental Idealism* had a profound influence on Blondel.

[14] It must be noted that in *L'action* (1893) Blondel did not use the term 'methode d'imminence'. It appeared for the first time in his *Le Lettre* (1896) which was an apologetic letter written to philosophers and theologians who were critical of his theory.

[15] Jean Lacroix, *Maurice Blondel: An Introduction to the Man and his Philosophy*, tr. John C. Guiness (New York: Sheed & Ward, 1968) 26.

[16] Blondel was a much older contemporary of Teilhard de Chardin. Chardin began writing when Blondel was already in his retirement.

[17] In light of what we have said in the introduction, we may note that Blondel's philosophical theology poses a critical question to the dominant stream of Catholic theology, Thomistic Scholasticism. Some of Blondel's contemporaries who were identified as Modernists, like Desire Joseph Mercier, George Tyrrell, Baron von Hugel, Alfred Loisy, and Lucien Laborthoniere, had brought to light the poverty of Scholasticism. Some, notably Laborthoniere, vehemently attacked Scholasticism. Blondel, on the other hand, presented a viable alternative. According to Blondel, scholasticism posited two levels of reality--reason and faith, natural and supernatural. These realities were regarded as being superimposed. Blondel was convinced that they were not just a juxtaposition of parts but formed a real unity.

[18] John R. Staude, *Max Scheler: An Intellectual Portrait* (New York: The Free Press, 1967), 1.

[19] This work was written in 1928. The English translation is entitled *Man's Place in the Universe*. It was intended by Scheller as a prelude to an elaborate work on his philosophical anthropology.

[20] See John Macquarrie, *Twentieth Century Religious Thought: The Frontiers of Philosophy and Theology 1900-1970* (London: SCM Press, 1973), 220-223.

[21] He speaks of 5 dominant types in history: *Homo religiosus, Homo sapiens, Homo faber,* man as the failure of 'life' and man as the *Ubermensch.*

[22] Max Scheler, *Man's Place in Nature*, tr. Hans Meyerhoff, (New York: Noonday Press, 1961),3.

[23] I retain the term 'man' here to be true to Scheler's use of that term.

[24] Meyendorff, in the Preface to Max Scheler, *Man's Place in Nature,* xxxv.

[24] Ibid., 93.

[25] Ibid., 93.

[26] Ibid., 6.

[27] F. LeRon Shults, "Integrative Epistemology and the Search for Meaning," in *Journal of Interdisciplinary and Interfaith Dialogue*, 1993, Vol V No1/2, 125.

[28] Ibid., 125.

[29] Ibid., 127.

[30] Oskar Gruenwal, "The Unity of the Arts and Sciences: Pathways to God's creation," in *Journal of Interdisciplinary and Interfaith Dialogue*, 1993, Vol V No1/2, 2.

[31] Alexandre Ganoczy, "Dualism" in *Systematic Theology: Roman Catholic Perspectives*, eds. Francis Schussler Fiorenza and John P. Galvin (Minneapolis: Fortress Press, 1991), 191-192.

[32] The words of Aquinas, "*Gratia supponit naturam et perficit illam*" give a clear notion of his understanding of the relationship between nature and grace.

[33] Georg Kraus, "Nature and Grace," in *Systematic Theology: Roman Catholic Perspectives*, 504.

[34] Rita Gross, "Androcentrism and Androgyny in the Methodology of History of Religions," in *Beyond Androcentrism: New Essays on Women and Religion* (Missoula, MT: Scholars Press, 1977), 9.

[35] Simone de Beauvoir, *The Second Sex* (New York: Bantam Books, 1961), xv.

[36] Elizabeth Schussler Fiorenza, *In Memory of Her: A Feminist Theological Reconstruction of Christian Origins* (New York, Crossroads, 1983), 108.

[37] Anne Carr, *Transforming Grace: Christian Tradition and Women's Experience* (San Francisco: Harper and Row, 1988), 46-49.

[38] Rosemary Radford Ruether, *Religion and Sexism: Images of Women in the Jewish and Christian Traditions* (New York: Simon and Schuster, 1974), 157-158.

[39] Other feminist theologians like Valerie Saiving, Carol Christ, Mary Daly, Elizabeth Johnson, Judith Plaskow, Anne Carr have also pointed out the poverty of a one-sided Christian anthropology.

[40] Georg Kraus, "Grace" in *Handbook of Catholic Theology*, eds. Wolfgang Beinert and Francis Schussler Fiorenza (New York, NY: The Crossroad Publishing Company, 1995), 308.

[41] Stephen Hawking, A Brief History of Time: From the Big Bang to Black Holes, (New York, NY: Bantam Books, 1988), 35-40.

[42] Dermot Lane, *Keeping Hope Alive: Stirrings in Christian Theology*, (New York, NY: Paulist Press, 1996),2.

[43] Ibid., ix.

[44] Ibid., 25-26.

CHAPTER II: SUBJECT AS SELF-TRANSCENDENT

[1] Robert Doran puts it thus: "But already it is clear that the work of few if any other twentieth-century thinkers has a comparable range of implications for various fields or a comparable importance for the future of thought and indeed of human living" ["Introduction: Lonergan: An Appreciation" in *The Desires of the Human Heart*, ed. Vernon Gregson (New York, NY: Paulist Press, 1988), 1]. And Brian Davies writes, "The range of his interests and the sheer intellectual force of his literary output cannot but command respect and interest in serious-minded thinkers concerned, not only with theology and philosophy, in which Lonergan specialized, but also with the human sciences and with human studies in general" in his editorial forward to F.E. Crowe, *Lonergan* (London: Biddles Ltd., 1992), vii.

[46] Gregson,*Desires of the Human Heart*, vi-vii.

[47] When I refer to Lonergan's earlier works, I am following the division that David Tracy outlines in *The Achievement of Bernard Lonergan* (New York: Herder and Herder, 1970). He explains that the later Lonergan for him "is not the Lonergan of his early works on Aquinas (*Gratia Operans* and *Verbum* articles) nor the Lonergan of his speculative treatises *De Deo Trino* and *De Verbo Incarnato* nor even the Lonergan of *Insight* but rather the Lonergan of his post-1957 work that work, in which the categories of historical consciousness and constitutive meaning have become his chief interest, methodology his chief question, and the technical category 'horizon' one of his chief theoretical tools." (p. 9)

[48] Gregson concurs with the division between the early and later Lonergan as suggested in this work. He writes, "the heart of the matter is, for the early Lonergan, the act of human understanding, and for the later Lonergan, the events that constitute intellectual, moral, and religious conversion." *Desires of the Human Heart*, 1.

[49] Lonergan's first published work was his doctoral work *St. Thomas' Thought on Gratia Operans* which appeared in "Theological Studies" 2, 3 in 1941-1942; the essays in *The Third Collection*, which was posthumously published in 1985, span the years 1974-82.

[50] Lonergan. *Understanding and Being: The Halifax Lectures on Insight*, eds. Elizabeth A. Morelli and Mark D. Morelli, 2nd edn; *Collected Works of Bernard Lonergan 5*, (Toronto: University of Toronto Press, 1990), xvii.

[51] Gregson, *Desires of the Human Heart*, vi-vii.

[52] Ibid., 107.

[53] Gregson, "The Desire to Know: Intellectual Conversion" in *The Desires of the Human Heart*, 26.

[54] This is what Lonergan sets to establish in his first major original work, *Insight: A Study of Human Understanding*, (London: Longmans, Green and Co, 1957). He offers a series of exercises by which one can arrive at insight through self-appropiation.

[55] Leibniz believed that reason was capable of unifying all sciences connecting philosophy and science, theology, morals and reason. Theoretical

intellect, he believed, could lead us to the knowledge of God. Kant, on the other hand, investigated whether or not human reason was capable of any metaphysical knowledge at all. Kant held that synthetic principles can not be obtained from sense data. This led him to expound *The Critique of Practical Reason and The Critique of Judgment.*

[56] *Understanding and Being*, 371.

[57] We find Lonergan dealing with Kant in the lectures he delivered in 1952 at Regis College, Toronto. These lectures were based on the notes in preparation for *Insight.* He addresses Kant in his 1968 Marquette lecture, *The Subject.* There are other references in the three Collections.

[58] Joseph Marechal was a Belgian Jesuit, who taught in Louvain. Marechal had written *Le Thomisme devant la Philosphie critique* and *La Critique de Kant.* Lonergan admits that his knowledge of Marechal was largely acquired by osmosis, as he had learned it from Stephanos Stephanou, an Athenian Jesuit from the Sicilian Province who had studied in Louvain. Lonergan was well aware, as he himself notes in "Discussion 4" in *Understanding and Being* that Marechal was "a recognized commentator of Kant."

[59] Joseph de Tonquedec was a French Jesuit. He had worked out a theory of knowledge in terms of looking and confronting. For him, knowing is looking. Lonergan points out that he [Lonergan] has a problem with de Tonquedec's treatment of knowledge in conjunction with judgment.

[60] *Understanding and Being*, 179.

[61] David Tracy, *The Achievement of Bernard Lonergan,*94.

[62] See *Understanding Being*, 297-299.

[63] *Understanding and Being*, 297.

[64] Ibid., 299.

[65] Ibid.

[66] *Method*, 95-96.

[67] Lonergan, "Mission and Spirit" in *A Third Collection: Papers by Bernard J.F. Lonergan*, ed. Frederick E. Crowe, (New York: Paulist, 1985), 28.

[68] "A Post-Hegelian Philosophy of Religion," in *A Third Collection*, 207-208.

[69] Lonergan gave this as the Aquinas Lecture at Marquette University in 1968 under the auspices of the Wisconsin-Alpha Chapter of *Phi Sigma Tau.*

[70] Lonergan, *The Subject*, 5.

[71] Ibid., 2.

[72] Ibid., 3.

[73] Ibid., 7.

[74] Ibid.

[75] Ibid., 8.

[76] Ibid., 9.

[77] Ibid., 12.

[78] Ibid., 17.

[79] Ibid., 20.

[80] *Method*, 6.

[81] Ibid., 6-8.

[82] *Understanding and Being*, 15-16.
[83] Ibid., 33.
[84] Ibid., 14.
[85] *The Subject*, 20-21.
[86] *Method*, 9.
[87] Ibid., 14-15.
[88] We will return to the notion of sublation in Lonergan in Chapter four when we explore conversions. However, it is important to bring some clarity to Lonergan's use of this term. In *Method*, he writes, "I would use this notion [sublation] in Karl Rahner's sense rather than Hegel's to mean that what sublates goes beyond what is sublated, introduces something new and distinct, puts everything on a new basis, yet so far from interfering with the sublated or destroying it, on the contrary needs it, includes it, reserves all its proper features and properties, and carries them forward to a fuller realization within a richer context (p.241)."
[89] *Method*, 9.
[90] Ibid.
[91] Ibid.
[92] Ibid.
[93] Lonergan, like Aristotle and Aquinas before him, maintained that all questions a person can raise can be characterized as '*Quid sit?*' (What is it), '*An sit?*'(Is it true?), '*Cur ita sit*' (Why is it true?) and '*An ita Sit?*' Tracy commenting on this, writes, "It is the pure activity of questioning that most adequately reveals the dynamics of intelligence and rationality, For every authentic question involves a heuristic anticipation of the unknown (the questionable) that is in some way already known (as questioned)." *The Achievement*, 126.
[94] Ibid.
[95] Ibid., 11-12.
[96] Tracy, *The Achievement of Bernard Lonergan*, 212.
[97] *Method*, 81.
[98] Tracy, *The Achievement of Bernard Lonergan*, 209-210.
[99] *Method*, 76.
[100] Ibid., 76-77.
[101] Ibid., 77.
[102] Tracy, *The Achievement of Bernard Lonergan*, 210.
[103] Ibid., 211.
[104] Ibid.
[105] *Method*, 81.
[106] Ibid., 57.
[107] Ibid., 59.
[108] Ibid., 64.
[109] Tracy, *The Achievement of Bernard Lonergan*, 213.
[110] *Method*, 64-65.

CHAPTER III: PERSON AS MEANING-MAKER

[111] Robert Kegan, *The Evolving Self*, Preface.

[112] *Ibid.*

[113] Ibid., 72.

[114] Jean-Claude Bringuier, *Conversations with Jean Piaget* tr. Basia Miller Gulati Chicago: University of Chicago Press, 1980) 36-48. This particular conversation took place in 1969. Though Piaget agreed to the term 'structuralism,' he was quick to point out that popular notion of structuralism conveyed something static as in a solid structure. His understanding was developmental.

[115] Hugh Rosen, *The development of Sociomoral Knowledge: A Cognitive-Structural Approach*, (New York: Columbia University Press, 1980) 105.

[116] As this chapter is intended to present Kegan's theory, I refrain from making any explicit reference to Lonergan in the course of this chapter. However, it is important to footnote here what Kegan and Lonergan share when it pertains to their epistemological underpinnings to their respective theories. In the previous chapter, we have explained in some detail how Lonergan, in working out his theory of knowledge, refuted the extremes of empiricism and rationalism. It is significant that Kegan, as did Piaget before him, thoroughly rejects rationalism (that ideas are innate as was held by Plato, Spinoza, and Leibniz) on the one hand, and empiricism (that the mind is a *tabula rasa* held by Locke, Berkeley, and Hume) on the other hand.

[117] *The Evolving Self*, 26.

[118] Heinz Werner, *Comparative Psychology of Mental Development* (New York, NY: International Universities Press, 1940).

[119] Robert Kegan, et al., "Life After Formal Operations: Implications for a Psychology of the Self" in *Theories of Higher Stages of Consciousness and Self-Development*, 230.

[120] Ibid., 231.

[121] *The Evolving Self*, 26.

[122] Ibid., 12.

[123] *The Evolving Self*, 4.

[124] Ibid., 8.

[125] Ibid., 9.

[126] Robert Kegan, et al., "Life After Formal Operations: Implications for a Psychology of the self" in *Theories of Higher Stages of Consciousness and Self-Development*, 229.

[127] Ibid, 229.

[128] Robert Kegan, *The Evolving Self*, Preface.

[129] Ibid., 10.

[130] Ibid., 83.

[131] Robert G. Kegan and Gil G. Noam, "On Boundaries and Externalizations" in *Psychoanalytic Inquiry*, 404.

[132] *The Evolving Self*, 113.

[133] Ibid., 8.

[134] Ibid.

[135] Ibid.

[136] Kegan maintains that the self is both the organizing entity as well as the process of organizing. Michael D. Berzonsky, who formulated a social-cognitive model of identity development, also considers ego identity as a process and a product. However, much like William James, Berzonsky subscribes to a dualistic conception of the self-as-knower and self-as-known. See *Discussion on Ego Identity*, ed. Jane Kroger (Hillsdale, N.J.: L. Erlbaum, 1993), 169.

[137] *The Evolving Self*, viii-ix

[138] *In Over Our Heads*, 313

[139] Ibid., 116.

[140] Ibid., 121.

[141] Kegan alludes to this in *The Evolving Self*, 107.

[142] *The Evolving Self*, 129.

[143] In this book, Kegan uses the backdrop of Martin Buber's philosophy to present some of the works of two Jewish writers, Saul Bellow and Bernard Malamud as offering a new voice for contemporary fiction.

[144] Kegan writes in the Prologue to *In Over Our Heads*, "The theory's central premises and distinctions remain unchanged, but they are clearer and better supported. The principles of mental organization according to which emotional, cognitive, interpersonal, and parts of ourselves and our relationship to others, are explicated here rather than merely claimed" (p.7).

[145] Ibid., 114.

[146] Ibid., 114.

[147] Ibid., 114.

[148] Robert G. Kegan and Gil G. Noam. "On Boundaries and Externalizations" in *Psychoanalytic Inquiry*, 3, 1989, 405.

[149] *The Evolving Self*, 88.

[150] Ibid., 138.

[151] Ibid., 139.

[152] Robert G. Kegan and Gil G. Noam. "On Boundaries and Externalizations" in *Psychoanalytic Inquiry*, 405-6.

[153] Ibid., 406.

[154] *The Evolving Self*, 90.

[155] Ibid., 94.

[156] *The Evolving Self*, 97.

[157] Ibid., 100.

[158] Ibid., 101.

[159] Ibid., 102.

[160] Ibid., 104.

[161] Ibid., 113.

[162] Ibid., 105.

[163] Ibid., 104.

[164] Ibid., 104.

[165] *In Over Our Heads*, 5.

[166] Ibid., 11.

141

[167] Ibid., 7.

[168] *Evolving Self*, 83.

[169] *In Over Our Heads*, 29.

[170] Carol Gilligan critiqued Lawrence Kohlberg's stage theory of moral development, which takes justice as the norm of morality. Gilligan's research indicates that while boys and men are focused on duty and responsibility, girls and women are involved in a web of relationships. A deontological morality based on duty, Gilligan argues, should not be held as the norm for women.

[171] *Evolving Self*, 109.

[172] *In Over Our Heads*, 203.

[173] *Evolving Self*, 108-9.

[174] Ibid., 107.

CHAPTER IV: SELF-TRANSCENDING MEANING-MAKER

[175] *Method*, 13.

[176] *Collection*, 243.

[177] Frederick Crowe convincingly argues that Lonergan comes in the line of Aristotle and Bacon who had provided organons for their own times. This claim is very evident even in the title of his book, *Method in Theology: An Organon for our Time*, (Milwaukee, WI: Marquette University Press, 1980)

[178] Kegan has demonstrated the balances of self and other as the common ground of the above theories in a table format. This helps us to verify Kegan's claim of providing a unifying perspective. For the table, see *Evolving Self*, 86-87.

[179] *Sweeter Welcome*, 13.

[180] Albert Camus. *The Myth of Sisyphus and other Essays*, New York, NY: Vintage, 1955), 91.

[181] *The Sweeter Welcome*, 16

[182] Ibid.

[183] Ibid., p.10.

[184] *The Sweeter Welcome*, 5.

[185] Ibid.

[186] Ibid.

[187] Ibid.,16.

[188] Harvey Cox, *The Secular City*, (New York, NY: Macmillan, 1965), 16.

[189] William Barrett, *Irrational Man*,(New York, NY: Doubleday,1958), 78.

[190] Barrett, 78.

[191] *The Sweeter Welcome*, 18.

[192] Martin Buber, *Hasidism and the Modern Man* tr. Maurice Friedman (New York: Horizon Press, 1958), 49.

[193] Ibid., 32-33.

[194] Buber, *Mamre, Essays in Religion by Martin Buber*, tr. Greta Hort, Melbourne: Melbourne University Press, 1946), 78.

[195] Kegan, *The Evolving Self*, viii-ix.

[196] *Insight*, ix-xv.

[197] Tracy, *The Achievement of Bernard Lonergan*, 104.

[198] We must note that when Tracy was writing this book, he only had the manuscript at his disposal for Lonergan's *Method in Theology*.

[199] Tracy *The Achievement*, 9.

[200] Walter Conn, *Conscience--Development and Self-Transcendence*, Birmingham, Ala.: Religious Education Press, 1981), 195-196.

[201] Lonergan, *Method*, 235.

[202] Michael Novak, "The Christian and the Atheist" in Bernard Murchland (ed.), *The Meaning of the Death of God* (New York: Vintage Books, 1967), 77.

[203] Lonergan, *Method*, 237.

[204] Ibid.

[205] Conn, *Conscience*, 129.

[206] Tracy, *Achievemnt*, 10.

[207] *Method.*, 236.

[208] Lonergan, "Theology in Its Context" *Theology of Renewal* (New York: Herder and Herder, 1968) Vol. I, 38.

[209] There has been a discussion about affective conversion as being distinct from moral conversion and, consequently, deserving of separate attention. Lonergan acknowledged affective conversion but found moral conversion to be inclusive of affective conversion. There have been questions regarding whether Christian conversion is distinct from religious conversion. Are moral and religious conversions two disctinct conversions? Can there be a true religious conversion without a authentic moral conversion? We shall restrict our discussion here to the three that Lonergan usually referred to: intellectual, moral, and religious conversions.

[210] Ibid., 237-238.

[211] Ibid., 237-244.

[212] Conn, *Concscience*, 180

[213] Tracy, *Achievement*, 231.

[214] *Method*, 238.

[215] Ibid., 239-240.

[216] Ibid., 231.

[217] Richard Liddy, *Transforming Light: Intellectual Conversion in Early Lonergan* (Collegeville, MN: Liturgical Press, 1993) 198.

[218] Walter Conn, "The Desire for Authenticity: Conscience and Moral Conversion" in Vernon Gregson,ed. *The Desires of the Human Heart,* 36.

[219] *Method*, 16.

[220] It is important to point out that the drive to transcendence, according to Lonergan, may be thwarted in a human subject. Already in *Insight* (pp. 191-194), Lonergan had spoken of the possibility of the subject to refuse insight. He called this 'bias.' We have not explored the negative possibilities in our work. However, the acceptance of finitude as a datum of human experience in this framework leaves this theme open for future discussions.

[221] Conn, "The Desire for Authenticity: Conscience and Moral Conversion" in *The Desires of the Human Heart,* 36.

[222] Donald J. Dorr in "Conversion" in *Looking at Lonergan's Method* ed. Patrick Corcoran (Dublin: the Talbot Press, 1975) makes this salient comment: "The book *Insight* might be fairly accurately described as an account of, and an invitation to, intellectual conversion.; and it contains as well important material on moral conversion—some of which (for instance the sections on bias) are referred to frequently when morality is being treated in *Method*" (p. 175).

[223] *Insight*,598-599.

[224] Liddy, 198.

[225] Liddy, *Transforming Light*. 198.

[226] Conn, *Conscience*, 179.

[227] See footnote no. 204 above.

[228] *Method*, 240.

[229] Conn, "The Desire for authenticity: Conscience and Moral Conversion." in *The Desires of the Human Heart*, 54.

[230] *Method*, 241.

[231] Ibid.

[232] *Method*, 240.

[233] Denise Lardner Carmody, "The Desire for Transcendence: Religious Conversion" in *The Desires of the Human Heart* ed. Vernon Gregson (New York: Paulist Press, 1988) 61.

[234] *Method*, 242.

[235] Lonergan cautions that it would be wrong to hold that because intellectual conversion is experienced first, it is to be regarded as the first conversion. His argument is that God's gift of His love precedes all else and hence, religious conversion is what makes the other two possible.

[236] Ibid., 241.

[237] Ibid.

[238] Lonergan explains his position in "Bernard Lonergan Responds" in *Foundations of Theology* ed. Patrick McShane (Dublin: Gill and Macmillan Ltd., 1971). He writes, "In order of exposition I would prefer to explain first the intellectual, then moral, then religious conversion...In order of occurrence I would expect religious commonly but not necessarily to precede moral and both religious and moral to precede intellectual" 233-234.

[239] See Martin Buber, *Hasidism and Modern Man*, 29-33.

[240] See *Method*, 240-241.

CHAPTER V: HUMAN EXISTENCE: THE EVER-UNFOLDING MYSTERY OF GRACE IN EXILE

[241] LeRon Shults, "Integrative Epistemology and the Search for Meaning," in *The Journal of Interdisciplinary Studies: an International Journal of Interdisciplinary and interfaith Dialogue*, 1993, Vol. V No, 1/2. 125.

[242] *Method*, 13.

[243] *Understanding and Being*, 33.

[244] Tracy, *Achievement of Lonergan*, 212.

[245] *Method*, 80-85.

[246] *The Evolving Self*, 94.

[247] Tracy, *Achievement of Lonergan*, 206-217.

[248] *The Sweeter Welcome*,16.

[249] Michael Novak, "The Christian and the Atheist," in *The Meaning of the Death of God*, ed. Bernard Murchland New York: Vintage Books, 1967), 77.

[250] The references are for the most part from the Priestly source and we can say that at least from the Post-exilic period the notion of human beings created in God's image seems to have been widely accepted among the Jewish thinkers.

[251] Melinda Johanning, *Some Aspects of the Image of God in Man in the Works of Origen and Gregory of Nyssa*, Master's thesis (Marquette University, Milwaukee, 1965), 3.

[252] M. Lot-Borodine, "La doctrine de la 'deification' dans l'Eglise greque jusq'au Xie seicle," *Revue de l'histoire des religions*, 105 (1932), 25.

[253] Johanning, 11.

[254] George A. Maloney, *Man the Divine Icon* (Pecos, NM: Dove Publications, 1973), 2.

[255] Johanning, 9.

[256] Ibid.

[257] Maloney, 39.

[258] David Cairns, *The Image of God in Man*, rev. ed.(London: Collins, 1973), 80ff.

[259] Maloney, 39.

[260] Anthony Hoekema, *Created in God's Image* (Grand Rapids, MI: Eerdmans, 1986), 33-35. Hoekema maintains that Irenaeus was wrong in distinguishing between the terms image and likeness, because in his opinion the two terms are synonyms. However, he also agrees that this distinction was part of the teaching tradition in the Middle Ages.

[261] We must note here that we are moving from the teaching of St. Irenaeus to that of Origen without presenting the theme in St. Clement of Alexandria. The reason for the omission is that though the thinking of Clement is significant in the larger discussion of the image of God theology, for our purpose here and for sake of conciseness, we are not dealing with the thinking of Clement in regard to the image of God or *theosis*.

[262] Johanning, 25-28.

[263] Maloney, 68.

[264] Ibid., 70.

[265] Ibid., 88.

[266] Ibid., 89-90.

[267] Ibid., 92. Maloney depends on Regis Bernard's work, *L'Image de Dieu d'apres Saint Athanase*, (Paris:Cerf, 1952).

[268] The Cappodocian Fathers, Basil the Great, Gregory Nazianzen and Gregory of Nyssa who played an important role in the ecumenical councils of

Nicaea and Constantinople have a strong theology of the image of God; however, they for the most part, reiterate the positions of the early Fathers we have discussed. An elaborate discussion of the way they present the doctrine of the image of God is not needed here for our purpose.

[269] Mark O'Keefe, *Becoming Good, Becoming Holy: On the Relationship of Christian Ethics and Spirituality*, (New York: Paulist Press, 1995).

[270] Ibid., 60.

[271] Ibid., 57.

[272] G. W. Butterworth, "The Deification of man in Clement of Alexandria." *Journal of Theological Studies* 17 (1916), 163.

[273] Keith Norman, *Deification: The content of Athanasian Soteriology*, Doctoral Work, Duke University (Ann Arbor, MI: University Microfims International, 1980) 26.

[274] Keith Norman provides a fuller development of the theme of *theosis* in the New Testament in 25-39.

[275] O'Keefe, 68-69.

[276] Norman, 38.

[277] O'Keefe, 60. O'Keefe cites several authors in his footnote that develop this theme more fully.

[278] Norman, 54.

[279] Irenaeus, *Adversus Haereses* IV, 38,4; V, 9, 2. As cited in Maloney, 99.

[280] Norman points out that humans are made "*capax incorruptonis et immortalitatis.*" Humans have been created to share in God's own incorruptibility and immortality.

[281281] Ibid., 57.

[282] Ibid., 61.

[283] The same can be said of Clement of Alexandria who was the first to use the term *theopoesis* to speak of the deifying action of the Incarnate Word in the Christian.

[284] Norman, 68-69.

[285] Origen, *On First Principles* as cited in Norman, *Deification*, 69.

[286] Johanning, 95.

[287] Maloney, 100.

[288] Ibid.

[289] Norman, 92.

[290] Athanasius, *Discourse against the Arians* II.74 as cited in Norman, *Deification*, 98.

[291] See Maloney, 99-102 and Norman, 92-106.

[292] Maloney, 103.

[293] Athanasius, *Against the Arians* as cited in Maloney, 100.

[294] Maloney, 99. Norman also highlights the significant role that the Holy Spirit plays in deification. See 126-130.

[295] Johanning, 13.

[296] See Chapter 1 Section 7.1.4. of this work.

[297] Gregson, *The Desires of the Human Heart*, 18.

[298] Lonergan, *Method*, 13.

[299] Ibid., 39.

[300] Gregson, 16-17.

[301] Lonergan, *Method,* 103.

[302] Lonergan, *Subject,* 22.

[303] Lonergan, *Mission and Spirit,* 32-33.

BIBLIOGRAPHY

Primary Sources:

Kegan, Robert. The Sweeter Welcome: Voices for a Vision of Affirmation--Bellow, Malamud, and Martin Buber, Needhjam Heights, Mass.: Humanitas Press, 1976.

------------. The Evolving Self: Problem and Process in Human Development, Cambridge, Mass.: Harvard University Press, 1982.

------------ and Gil, Noam G. "On Boundaries and Externalization: Clinical-Developmental Perspectives" 397-426 Psychoanalytic Inquiry 3, 1989.

------------ and Henderson, Ann, F. "Learning and Knowing, and the Self: A Constructive Developmental View" 267-303 in Learning and Education: Psychoanalytic Perspectives Madison, CT: International University Press, 1989.

------------. "Life after Formal Operations: Implications for a Psychology of the Self" 229-257 in Charles N. Alexander and Ellen J. Langer (eds.) Higher Stages of Human Development: Perspectives on Adult Growth, New York, NY: Oxford University Press, 1990.

------------ and Rogers, Laura. "Mental Growth and Mental Health as Distinct Concepts in the Study of Developmental Psychopathology" 103-147 in Constructivist Perspectives on Developmental Psychopathology and Atypical Development Hillsdale, NJ: Lawrence Erlbaum Associates, 1991.

------------. "The Evolution of Moral Meaning-Making" in Arthur Dobrin (ed.) Being Good and Doing Right 15-35, Lanham, MD: University Press of America,1993.

------------. In Over Our Heads: The Mental Demands of Modern Life, Cambridge, Mass.: HarvardUniversity Press, 1994.

Lonergan, Bernard J. F. De Constitutione Christi: Ontologica et Psychologica, Rome: Gregorian University, 1956.

------------. "Cognitional Structure" 530-542 Continuum 2, 1964.

------------. De Verbo Incarnato, Rome: Gregorian University, 1964.

--------------. Collection Papers by Bernard Lonergan, ed. F. E. Crowe, New York: Herder and Herder, 1967.

--------------. The Subject, Milwaukee: Marquette University Press, 1968.

--------------. "Religious Commitment" in J. Papin The Pilgrim People, 1970.

--------------. "Social Science and Theology" 280-282 Social Compass 17, 1970.

--------------. Grace and Freedom: Operative Grace in the Thought of St Thomas Aquinas, ed. J. Patout Burns with an introduction by F. E. Crowe, London: Darton, Longman and Todd, New York: Herder and Herder, 1971.

--------------. Method in Theology, ed. Seabury, Minneapolis, Minn: Seabury Press, 1979, c1972.

--------------. "Revolution in Catholic Theology" in Catholic Theological Society of America Proceedings, 1972.

--------------. Philosophy of God and Theology, Philadelphia: Westminster Press, 1973.

--------------. A Second Collection: Papers, (ed.) William F. J. Ryan and Bernard J. Tyrrell, London: Darton, Longman and Todd, 1974.

--------------. Bernard Lonergan: Three Lectures, (ed.) Eric O'Connor, Montreal: Thomas More Institute for Adult Education, 1975.

--------------. "Mission et l'Esprit" in P. Brand et al., (eds.) L'Experience de l'Esprit, 1976.

--------------. "Theology and Praxis" in Catholic Theological Society of America Proceedings, 1977.

--------------. "Religious Experience" in T. A. Dunne (ed.) Trinification of the World, 1978.

--------------. Insight: a Study of Human Understanding, rev. students edition, New York: Harper & Row, 1978.

--------------. Understanding and Being: An Introduction and Companion to Insight: The Halifax Lectures, ed. Elizabeth A. Morelli and Mark D. Morelli, New York: E. Mellen Press, c1980.

--------------. Creativity and Method: Essays in Honor of Bernard Lonergan, ed. Matthew L. Lamb, Milwaukee: Marquette University Press, 1981.

149

--------------. A Third Collection, ed. F. E. Crowe, New York: Paulist Press; London: G. Chapman, c1985.

-------------. "Theologie et Vie Spirituelle" 331-341 Science et Esprit 38, 1986.

--------------. Religion and Culture: Essays in Honor of Bernard Lonergan, ed. Timothy P. Fallon and Philip Boo Riley, Albany, N.Y.: State University of New York Press, c1987.

Secondary Sources:

Amy, William O. and James B Recob. Human Nature in the Christian Tradition, Washington DC: University Press of America, 1992.

Ashbrook, James B. The Human Mind and the Mind of God: Theological Promise in Brain Research, Lanham, MD: University Press of America, 1984.

Barrett, William. Irrational Man, New York: Doubleday, 1958.

Beavoir, Simone de. The Second Sex, New York: Bantam Books, 1961.

Beinert, Wolfgang and Francis Schussler Fiorenza. (eds.) Handbook of Catholic Theology New York: Crossroad Publishing company, 1995.

Boden, Margaret A. Jean Piaget, New York: Penguin Press, 1980.

Boer, Harry R. An Ember Still Glowing: Humankind as the Image of God, Grand Rapids, MI: Eerdmans Publishing Company, 1990.

Bouillard, Henri. Blondel and Christianity, Washington: Corpus Books, 1969.

Breen, Dorothy D. and Margaret C. Burnett. "Moral Dilemmas of Early Adolescents of Divorced and Intact Families: A Qualitative and Quantitative Analysis" 168-182 Journal of Early Adolescents 13, 1993.

Bringuier, Jean-Claude. Conversations Bith Jean Piaget tr. Basia Miller Gulati, Chicago: University of Chicago Press, 1980.

Brooks, Peter (ed.), Christian Spirituality, Bloomsbury, London: SCM Press, 1975.

Buber, Martin. Mamre, Essays in Religion by Martin Buber, tr. Greta Hort, Melbourne: Melbourne University Press, 1946.

--------------. I and Thou, tr. Ronald Gregor Smith, New York: Scribner, 1958.

150

--------------. Hasidism and the Modern Man. Tr. Maurice Friedman, New York: Horizon Press, 1966, c.1958.

--------------. The Eclipse of God: Studies in the relation between Religion and Philosophy, Atlantic Hights, N.J.: Humanities Press International, 1988.

Buhler, Pierre. Humain a l'Image De Dieu, Geneve: Editions Labor et Fides, 1989.

Burns, Patout J. (ed.), Theological Anthropology, Philadelphia, Fortress Press, 1981.

Butterworth, G.W. "The Deification of man in Clement of Alexandria," Journal of Theological Studies, 1916, v.17.

Cairns, David. The Image of God in Man, London: SCM Press, 1963.

Camus, Albert. The Myth of Sysyphus and Other Essays, New York: Vintage Books, 1955.

Carlsen, Mary B. Meaning-Making: Therapeutic Processes in Adult Development New York, NK: W. W. Norton, 1988.

Carr, Anne E. Transforming Grace: Christian Tradition and Women's Experience, San Francisco: Harper & Row, 1988.

Childs, James M. Jr. Christian Anthropology and Ethics, Philadelphia: Fortress Press, 1978.

Conn, Walter E.(ed). Conversion, Perspectives on Personal and Social Transformation, New York: Alba House, 1978.

--------------. Conscience--Development and Self-Transcendence, Birmingham, Ala.: Religious Education Press, 1981.

--------------. Christian Conversion: A Developmental Interpretation of Autonomy and Surrender, New York: Paulist Press, 1986.

Cooper, John W. Body, Soul, and Everlasting Life: Biblical Anthropology and the Monism-Dualism Debate, Grand Rapids, MI: Eerdmans, 1989.

Corcoran, Patrick. ed. Looking at Lonergan's Method, Dublin: Talbot Press, 1975.

Cox, Harvey. The Secular City, New York: Macmillan, 1965.

Crowe, F. E. Appropriating the Lonergan Idea, ed. Michael Vertin, Washington, D.C.: Catholic University of America Press, 1989.

--------------. Lonergan, London, England: Geoffrey Chapman, 1992.

--------------. Method in Theology: An Organon for our Time, Milwaukee, Wis.: Marquette University Press, 1980.

--------------. The Lonergan Enterprise, Cambridge: Mass, 1980.

Curran, Charles. Catholic Moral Theology in Dialogue, Notre Dame, Ind.: Fides Publishers, 1982.

------------. Moral Theology: A Continuing Journey, Notre Dame, Ind.:University of Notre Dame Press, c. 1982.

------------. Directions in Fundamental Moral Theology, Notre Dame: University of Notre Dame Press, c. 1985.

Dijon-Mayence. Journee Maurice Blondel, Dijon: Centre de Recherche sur l'Image, le Symbol et le Mythe, 1988.

Doran, Robert M. Psychic Conversion and Theological Foundations: Toward a Reorientation of the Human Sciences, Chico, Calif.: Scholars Press, 1981.

------------. Subject and Psyche: Ricoeur, Jung, and the Search for Foundations, Washington: University Press of America, 1977.

Duska, Ronald F. Moral Development: A Guide to Piaget and Kohlberg, by Ronald Duska and Mariellen Whelan, New York: Paulist Press, 1975.

Dykstra, Craig R. Vision and Character: A Christian Educator's Alternative to Kohlberg, New York: Paulist Press, 1981.

Elkind, David and John H. Flavell (eds). Studies in Cognitive Development; Essays in honor of Jean Piaget, New York: Oxford University Press, 1969.

Evans, Richard I. Jean Piagaet, the Man and His Ideas. tr. by Eleanor Duckworth, New York: E. P. Dutton, 1973.

Fallon, Timothy P and Philip Boo Riley, (eds). Religion in Context: Recent studies in Lonergan, Lanham, MD: University Press of America, 1988.

Farrell, Thomas J. and Paul A. Soukup, (eds). Communication and Lonergan: Common Ground for Forging the New Age, Kansas City, MO: Sheed & Ward, 1993.

Ferrari, Jean. Recherches Blondeliennes, Dijon: Publication de l'Universite de Dijon, 1989.

Fichtner, Joseph. Man, the Image of God: A Christian Anthropology, New York: Alba House, 1978.

Fiorenza, Elizabeth Schussler. In Memory of Her: A Feminist Theologicsl Reconstruction of Christian Origins, New York: Crossroad, 1987.

Fiorenza, Francis Schussler and John P. Gavin. (eds). Systematic Theology: Roman Catholic Perspectives Minneapolis: Fortress Press, 1991.

Fuchs, Josef. Human Values and Christian Morality, tr. M.H. Heelan et al., Dublin: Gill and McMillan, 1970.

Geffre, Claude, Le Christianisme au risque de l'interpretation, Paris: Cerf, 1983.

Gilligan Carol. In a Different Voice: Psychological Theory and Women's Devlopment, Cambridge, Mass: Harvard University Press, 1982.

Graff, Ann O'Hara, (ed). In the Embrace of God: Feminist Approaches to Theological Anthropology, Maryknoll, NY: Orbis Books, 1995.

Gregson, Vernon. Longergan, Spirituality, and the Meeting of Religions; Foreword by Sebastian Moore, Lanham, MD.: University Press of America, 1985.

-------------- (ed). The Desires of the Human Heart: An Introduction to the Theology of Bernard Lonergan, New York: Paulist Press, 1988.

-------------- Bernard Lonergan and the Dialogue of Religions: A Foundational Study of Religion as Spirituality, Doctoral Thesis, Marquette University, 1978.

Gruenwald, Oskar (ed). The Unity of the Arts and Sciences: Pathways to God's Creation?, An International Journal of Interdisciplinary and Interfaith Dialogue, V.5 No.1/2, Santa Monica, CA: Institute for Interdisciplinary Research, 1993.

Guttierez, Gustavo. Liberation and Change, ed. Ronald H. Stone,Atlanta: John Knox Press, 1977.

Hamman, A. G. L'Homme, Image De Dieu, Paris: Desclee, 1987.

Haring, Bernard. Free and Faithful: Moral Theology for Clergy and Laity (3 vols) New York: Seabury Press, 1978.

Hawking, Stephen. A Brief History of Time: From Big Bang to Big Holes, New York: Bantam Books, 1988.

Hefner, Philip J. The Human Factor: Evolution, Culture, and Religion, Minneapolis: Fortress Press, 1993.

Hersh, Richard H. Promoting Moral Growth: From Piaget to Kohlberg, Richard H Hersh, Diana Pritchard Poalitto, Joseph Reimer, New York: Longman, 1979.

Hoekema, Anthony A. Created in God's Image, Grand Rapids, MI: Eerdmans Publishing Company, 1986.

Johanning, Melinda, M. Some Aspecats of the Image of God in Man in the Works of Origen and Gregory of Nyssa, (Master's Thesis), Milwaukee, WI: Marquette University, 1965.

Kohlberg, Lawrence. Moral Stages: A Current Formulationand a Responseto Critics, New York: Kargen, 1983.

---------------. The Psychology of Moral Development: The Nature and Validity of Moral Stages, San Francisco: Harper & Row, 1984.

Kroger, Jane. Ed., Discussion on Ego Identity, Hillsdale, N.J.: L. Erlbaum, 1993.

Kung, Hans. Church. Tr. Ray and Rosaleen Oekenden, New York: Sheed and Ward, 1967.

--------------. Does God Exist? An Answer for Today, tr. Edward Quinn, London: Collins, 1980.

Lacroix, Jean. Maurice Blondel: An Introduction to the Man and his Philosophy, tr. John C. Guiness, New York: Sheed and Ward, 1968.

Lamb, Matthew L. (ed) Creativity and Method: Essays in Honor of Bernard Lonergan, Milwaukee, WI: Marquette University Press, 1981.

Lane, Dermot. Keeping Hope Alive: Stirrings in Christian Theology, New York: Paulist Press, 1996.

Lang, Martin A. Acquiring our Image of God: The Emotional Basis for Religious Education, New York: Paulist Press, 1983.

Leavy, Stanley A. In the Image of God: A Psychonalyst's View, New Haven, CT: Yale University Press, 1988.

Liddy, Richard M. Transforming Light: Intellectual Conversion in the Early Lonergan, Collegeville, MN: Liturgical Press, 1993.

Lot-Borodine, Myrrha. La Deification de l'homme, Paris, Les Editions du Cerf, 1970.

Macquarrie, John. Principles of Christian Theology, New York: Charles Scribner's Sons, 1966.

----------------. In Search of Humanity: A Theological and Philosophical Approach, New York: Crossroad, 1982.

Maier, Henry W. Three Theories of Child Development: The Contributions of Erik H. Erikson, Jean Piaget, and Robert R. Sears. and their Applications, New York: Harper & Row, 1969.

Maloney, George. Man the Divine Icon, Pecos, NM: Dove Publications, 1973.

May, Rollo. Man's Search for Himself, New York: WW Norton & Company, 1953.

McAuliffe, Garrett J. "Constructive Development and Career Transition: Implications for Counseling" 23-28 Journal of Counseling and Development 72, 1993.

McDonagh, Enda. Doing the Truth: The Quest for Moral Theology, Notre Dame, Ind.:University of Notre Dame, c. 1979.

-----------. Moral Theology Renewed: Papers of the Maynooth Union Summer School 1964, ed. Enda McDonagh, Dublin: Gill and Sons, 1965.

McGrane, Bernard. Beyond Anthropology: Society and the Other, New York: Columbia University Press, 1989.

McNeill, John J. The Blondelian Synthesis, Leiden, Netherlands: E.J. Brill, 1966.

Mcquarrie John R. Twentieth Century Religious Thought: The Frontiers of Philosophy and Theology 1900-1970, London: SCM Press, 1973.

McShane, Philip (ed). Foundations of Theology, (International Lonergan Congress, 1970, v.1), Notre Dame, IN: University of Notre Dame Press, 1972.

----------------. Language, Truth, and Meaning (International Lonergan Congress, 1970, v.2), Notre Dame, IN: University of Notre Dame Press, 1972.

Meynell, Hugo Anthony. An Introduction to the Philosophy of Bernard Lonergan, New York: Barnes & Noble Books, 1976.

Mooney, Christopher F. Man Without Tears: Soundings for a Christian Anthropology, New York: Harper & Row, 1975.

Mouroux, Jean. The Meaning of Man, Garden City, NY: Image Books, 1948.

Mullen, Peter F. "Gestalt Therapy and Constructive Developmental Psychology" 69-90 Gestalt Journal 13, 1990.

Munsey, Brenda (ed). Moral Development, Moral Education, and Kohlberg: Basics Issues in Philosophy, Psychology, Religion, and Education, Birmingham, Ala.: Religious Education Press, 1980.

Novak, Michael. "The Christian and the Atheist," in The Meaning of the Death of God ed. Bernard Murchland, New York: Vintage Books, 1967.

Norman, Keith E. Deification: The Content of Athanasian Soteriology, Doctoral Work, Ann Arbor, MI: University Microfilms International, 1980.

O'Callaghan, Michael C. Unity In Theology: Lonergan's Framework for Theology in its New Context, Washington, D.C.: University Press of America, 1980.

O'Keefe, Mark. Becoming Good, Becoming Holy: On the Relationship of Christin Ethics and Spirituality, New York: Paulist Press, 1995.

Pannenberg, Wolfhart. Human Nature, Election, and History, Philadelphia: Westminster Press, 1977.

Perico, Yvette. Maurice Blondel: Genese du sens, Campin, Belgique: Editions Universitaires, 1991.

Piaget, Jean. The Moral Judgement of the Child. tr. by Marjorie Warden, Glencoe, Ill., Free Press, 1932.

--------------. Judgement and Reasoning in the Child. In collaboration with E Cartalis and Others. Tr. by Marjorie Warden, London: Routledge & K. Paul, 1951.

--------------. The Essential Piaget, ed. Howard E. Guber, J. Jacques Voneche, New York: Basic Books, 1977.

--------------. Biologie et Connaissance, Chicago: University of Chicago Press, 1971.

--------------. Adaptation vitale et psychologie de l'intelligence, Chicago: University of Chicago Press, 1980.

Plaskow, Judith. Sex, Sin and Grace: Women's Experience and the Theologies of Reinhold Niebuhr and Paul Tillich, New York: University Press of America, 1980.

Power, F. Clark. <u>Lawrence Kohlberg's Approach to Moral Education</u>, Power F. Clark, Ann Higgins, Lawrence Kohlberg, New York: Columbia University Press, 1989.

Pratt, Michael W. et al. "Four Pathways in the Analysis of Adult Development and Aging: Comparing Analyses of Reasoning about Personal Life Dilemma" 666-675 <u>Psychology and Aging</u> 6, 1991.

Rahner, Karl. <u>The Christian of the Future</u>, tr. W.J. O'Hara. New York: Herder & Herder, 1967.

------------. <u>Do You Believe in God?</u> Tr. Richard Strchan, New York: Paulist Press, 1969.

------------. <u>Foundations of Christian Faith: An Introduction to the Idea of Christianity</u>, New York: Crossroad, 1978.

Rende, Michael L. <u>The Development of Fr. Bernard Lonergan's Thought on the Notion of Conversion</u> (microform), University of Michigan, Ann Harbor, 1983.

Reinhard, Hans G. "Depression and Moral Identity in Adolescence" 104-125 <u>Acta Paedopsychiatrica</u> 53, 1990.

Ring, Nancy C. <u>Doctrine Within the Dialectic of Subjectivity and Objectivity: A Critical Study of the Positions of Paul Tillich and Bernard Lonergan</u>, San Francisco: Mellen Research University Press, 1991.

Robertson, John C. Jr. <u>The Loss and Recovery of Transcendence: The Will to Power and the Light of Heaven</u>, Allison Park, PA: Pickwick Publications, 1995.

Rosen, Hugh. <u>The Development of Sociomoral Knowledge: A Cognitive-Structural Approach</u>, New York: Columbia University Press, 1980.

Ruther, Rosemary Radford. <u>Religion and Sexism: Images of Women in the Jewish and Chrsitian Traditions</u>, Hey York: Simon and Schusster, 1974.

Ryan, Maura C. and Gale S. Robinson. "What does it mean? Making Sense of the Hospital Experience" 17-20 <u>Journal of Gerontological Nursing</u> 16, 1990.

Sachs, John Randall. <u>The Christian Vision of Humanity: Basic Christian Anthropology</u>, Collegeville, MN: Liturgical Press, 1991.

Sala Giovanni B. <u>Lonergan and Kant: Five Essays on Human Knowledge</u>, Toronto: Toronto University Press, 1994.

Scheler, Max. On the Eternal in Man, New York: Harper & Brothers, 1960.

------------. Man's Place in Nature, New York: The Noonday Press, 1961.

Schulman, Valerie L., Lillian, Restaino-Baumann, and Loretta Butler, eds. The Future of Piagetian Theory: Neo-Piagetians, New York, NY: Plenum Press, 1985.

Schilpp, Paul Arther and Maaurice Friedman. Eds. The Philosophy of Martin Buber, La Salle, Ill.: Open Court, 1962.

Schwarz, Hans. Our Cosmic Journey: Christian Anthropology in the Light of Current Trends in the Sciences, Philosophy, and Theology, Minneapolis: Augsburg Publishing House, 1977.

Shults, LeRon F. "Integrative Epistemology and the Search for Meaning," in Journal of Interdisciplinary and Interfaith Dialogue, 1993, Vol V No1/2.

Siirala, Aarne. Divine Humanness, Philadelphia, Fortress Press, 1970.

Sommerville, James M. Total Commitment: Blondel's L'Action, Washington: Corpus Books, 1968.

Staude, John. Max Scheler: An Intellectual Portrait, New York: The Free press, 1967.

Stebbins, Michael J., The Divine Initiative: Grace, World Order and Human Freedom in the Early Writings of Bernard Lonergan, Toronto, Buffalo: University of Toronto Press, 1995.

Tracy, David. The Achievement of Bernard Lonergan, New York: Herder and Herder, 1970.

-------------. Blessed Rage for Order: The New Pluralism in Theology, New York:Seabury Press, 1975.

Tyrrell, Bernard. Bernard Lonergan's Philosophy of God, Notre Dame, Ind.: University of Notre Dame Press, 1972.

Valerie L. Shulman et al (eds). The Future of Piagetian Theory: The Neo-Piagetians, New York: Plenum Press, 1985.

Van Leeuwen, Mary S. The Person in Psychology: A Contemporary Christian Appraisal, Grand Rapids,   MI: Eerdmans, 1985.

158

Vaughn, Connie M. and David T. Pfenninger. "Kelly and the Concept of Developmental Stages" 177-190 <u>Journal of Constructivist Psychology</u> 7, 1994.

Wadsworth, Barry J. <u>Piaget's Theory of Cognitive Development: An Introduction for Students of Psychology and Education</u>, New York: Longman, 1979.

Werner, Heinz. <u>Comparative Psychology of Menta Development</u>, New York: International Universities Press, 1948.

Wilfred, Drath H. "Managerial Strengths and Weaknesses as Functions of the Development of Personal Meaning" 483-499 <u>Journal of Applied Behavioral Science</u> 26, 1990.

Wren, Thomas E. et al. (eds) <u>The Moral Domain: Essays in the Ongoing Discussion between Philosophy and the Social Sciences</u>, ed.Cambridge, Mass.: MIT Press, 1990.

Zeno, Carl Arthur. <u>The Meaning of "Real" According to Bernard Lonergan</u> (microfilm), 1976.

159

INDEX

888

L'Action 6

Aeterni Patris 1

Aquinas, Thomas 21,28,31,85,108

Aristotle 23,28,31,36,85

Athanasius 120-121,125-126

Augustine 8,21-22,28,31

Beauvoir, Simone de 22

Bellow, Saul 87,89,114

Bergson, Henri 6,8,9

Berkeley, George 32

Blondel, Maurice 6-8,11,107

Bounded boundlessness 5,19,26

Buber, Martin 6,38,56,70,87,89-92,114

Camus, Albert 86,114

Chardin, Teihard de 6,8

Conn, Walter 2,19,93-94,98-101

Conscious and Intentional Operations
52,93,102,114

Conscious Operations 37,47,51,83,107

Constructive Developmentalism
13,62-63,65,67,84,112

Conversion 2,12,14,18-19,28-29,38,52,
55,57,83,92,96-104,110,113,115,132

Copernicus 24

Critique of Pure Reason 33

Curran, Charles 2

Darwin, Charles 24

Decentration 62

Deification 9-11,105,121-122,124-126

Descartes, Rene 23,31-32

Dialectical Context 68,110

Dichotomization 15,21

Dichotomous Choice 68,92

Die Stellung des Menschen im Kosmos
8-9

Disembeddedness 69-70,74,80,110,131

Ecotheology 25,129

Embeddedness 66,69-70,80,110,131

Empiricists 23,31-32,39-43,97,108

Equilibration 62,76

Erikson, Erik 19,37,60,63,65,76

Eschatology 25,26,129

Evolving Self 11,13-14,59,61,66,70-71,
78-80,85,87-88,91-92,110,112,114,130

Existential Subject 32,38,40-42,45-47,
83,107

Existential-Phenomenological Tradition
13,63

Faculty Psychology 3,26,31,106,128

Fowler, James 19,63,67

Freud, Sigmund 37,59-60,64,72

Fuchs, Josef 2

Galileo 24

Gaudium et Spes 1,2

Genetic Epistemology 13,18,109

Gilligan, Carol 79

Grace 2,5,20-24,26,55,101-102,105,
117,127-129,132

ROMAN CATHOLIC STUDIES

1. L. Thomas Snyderwine (ed.), **Researching the Development of Lay Leadership in the Catholic Church Since Vatican II: Bibliographical Abstracts**

2. Frank Przetacznik, **The Catholic Concept of Genuine and Just Peace as a Basic Collective Human Right**

3. Andrew Cuschieri, **Introductory Readings in Canon**

4. Ernest Skublics, **How Eastern Orthodoxy Can Contribute to Roman Catholic Renewal: A Theological and Pastoral Proposition**

5. Robert J. Kaslyn, **"Communion with the Church" and the Code of Canon Law: An Analysis of the Foundation and Implications of the Canonical Obligation to Maintain Communion with the Catholic Church**

6. Patricia Voydanoff and Thomas M. Martin (eds.), **Using a Family Perspective in Catholic Social Justice and Family Ministries**

7. Michael Sundermeier and Robert Churchill (eds.), **The Literary and Educational Effects of the Thought of John Henry Newman**

8. Ross A. Shecterle, **The Theology of Revelation of Avery Dulles, 1980-1994: Symbolic Mediation**

9. Filippo Maria Toscano, **El Universalismo Del Pensamiento Cristiano De Don Luigi Sturzo**

10. James L. MacNeil, **A Study of Gaudium et Spes 19-22, The Second Vatican Council Response to Contemporary Atheism**

11. David B. Perrin, **The Sacrament of Reconciliation: An Existential Approach**

12. Stephen R. Duncan, **A Genre in Hindusthani Music (Bhajans) as Used in the Roman Catholic Church**

13. Maria G. McClelland, **The Sisters of Mercy, Popular Politics and the Growth of the Roman Catholic Community in Hull, 1855-1930**

14. Robert Berchmans, **A Study of Lonergan's Self-Transcending Subject and Kegan's Evolving Self: A Framework for Christian Anthropology**